Undergraduate Topics in Computer Science

Undergraduate Topics in Computer Science (UTiCS) delivers high-quality instructional content for undergraduates studying in all areas of computing and information science. From core foundational and theoretical material to final-year topics and applications, UTiCS books take a fresh, concise, and modern approach and are ideal for self-study or for a one- or two-semester course. The texts are all authored by established experts in their fields, reviewed by an international advisory board, and contain numerous examples and problems. Many include fully worked solutions.

More information about this series at http://www.springer.com/series/7592

Bhim P. Upadhyaya

Programming with Scala

Language Exploration

 Springer

Bhim P. Upadhyaya
Carnegie Mellon University – Silicon Valley
NASA Ames Research Park
Bldg. 23, Moffett Field
CA 94035
USA

ISSN 1863-7310   ISSN 2197-1781   (electronic)
Undergraduate Topics in Computer Science
ISBN 978-3-319-69367-5   ISBN 978-3-319-69368-2   (eBook)
https://doi.org/10.1007/978-3-319-69368-2

Library of Congress Control Number: 2017955281

Printed on acid-free paper

This Springer imprint is published by Springer Nature
The registered company is Springer International Publishing AG
The registered company address is: Gewerbestrasse 11, 6330 Cham, Switzerland

To the United Nations
-Bhim

Preface

We are living in a very interesting time, in terms of technological advancements among other things. In the last 60 years, humanity has made tremendous progress in the field of computing. High level programming languages appeared in the late 1950s, but there were no microprocessors available. One can imagine how tedious it could be to program. With the invention of microprocessors in the late 1960s, this field got a great boost. Along with hardware developments, new high level programming languages started emerging. Among those are Pascal, Smalltalk, C, etc. Some of these languages are still widely used. One of the interesting facts about these high level languages is that they had niche application areas, even though they were widely projected as general purpose languages, including in the textbooks. For example, Pascal was leaning toward education, C was primarily developed to ease operating systems developments, Fortran was for scientific computing, etc. Whatever the domains, each of these languages has shaped the history of computing.

Today, shapes, sizes, and capacities of computing devices are much different than 60 years ago. In the last 20 years, computing has shifted from localized client-server environments to world wide client-server environments. There are several catalysts for this change, including the invention of the world wide web, the advancements in integrated circuits, and the innovations in device manufacturing. One of the catalysts, which doesn't get enough credit, is the advancements of programming languages. Developers are truly enabled by language innovations. The innovation that JVM brought, has greatly impacted software engineering in general, and Internet based applications development in particular. Being able to program, without worrying about incompatibilities with hundreds of vendor specific architectures, is a great relief for software engineers.

One of the important aspects of advancements, not discussed enough, in industrial settings is knowledge evolution. I have had the privilege of working for the world's largest (non-profit) organization, the United Nations, which gave me an opportunity to work with people from almost every major cultural background. Also I have worked for some of the largest and finest for-profit organizations in the world. In addition to this, I was fortunate enough to be part of some of the finest universities in the world, either through academic programs, or by working directly with academicians in unique settings. This experience allows me to make some inferences on knowledge evolution, specially in the field of software engineering. The first inference is that changing a programming language is not pleasant, specially for professional programmers. The second inference is that adapting a new language to the level that one can sell the skills has strong limitations. The third inference is that the popularity of a particular language is strongly affected by the industry–academic loop, directly or indirectly. To be precise, how a language is taught, where it is taught, what kind of learning materials are available, etc., determine how popular a language will become.

Dr. Martin Odersky, the creator of Scala, has done a great job of a language innovation. Scala not only provides an opportunity to program in multiple paradigms, but also makes developers more productive with today's computing infrastructure. Most of the earlier languages were not designed to program in distributed environments. Also most of them were not designed to evolve. One of the fascinating aspects of Scala is that it can be grown, based on developers' needs. Remember, for every genius, there is a limit to how many languages one can become expert in. It is pretty much like the case of natural languages. We can recall ourselves, how good we are in our mother tongue and how good we are in other languages. Do we struggle? The Scala creator has gifted a beautiful solution to the world of computer programmers.

With this book, I have tried to enrich the learning aspect of Scala. I strongly believe that Scala can be a great first programming language. There is no need to lean on any other programming language in order to learn it, except the environment, which is JVM for a good reason. The approach that I have taken in this book was primarily inspired by my first hand observations of how professional programmers master a new technology. Also it is partly influenced by my experience of teaching undergraduate computer science and engineering students, over half a decade. I have tried to present complete and runnable programs, whenever possible. In the last 12 years, I noticed professional programmers learning faster by tweaking existing programs. This was true for my undergraduate students as well. Tweaking allowed learners to build self-confidence, which I found was the basis for the majority of learners for their long term pursuits. This book can be used, both at an undergraduate level and at a graduate level, to teach a first programming course. Also it is a great companion for professional programmers planning to switch to Scala.

Each chapter has review questions to reinforce your learning, which makes you ready for problem solving. You will find yourself adequate and self-confident, thereby keeping you away from the path of frustration. I have seen many great professional programmers being frustrated while learning a new language. Also each chapter has problems to solve. These problems are much closer to what you will need when you embark on your career as a professional Scala programmer. The process of solving problems expands your knowledge boundary; you are moving from reinforcing to developing salable skills.

Sunnyvale, California   *Bhim P. Upadhyaya*
June 2017

Contents

List of Figures

List of Tables

Chapter 1
Introduction to Computing

The *Oxford English Dictionary* (OED) defines computing as "the use of operation of computers"; similarly, computation is defined as "the action of mathematical calculation." In daily life, we often find these words being used interchangeably even though the scientific community makes a distinction. Let's first analyze computation as it appeared first in human civilization, formally with the invention of numbers. It is quite self-evident that humans performed computation before inventing numbers, as there should be a thought process before finding suitable symbols for that thought process. This kind of thought process is likely to be available in other *Mammalias* as well as in some other *Classes*, categorized using traditional biological taxonomy.

Let's take two examples to illustrate computation: $1 + 1 = 2$ and $13 + 29 = 42$. Now, let's ask ourselves these questions: *What percentage of the world population can perform first addition? What percentage of the world population can perform second addition without using a calculating machine? What percentage of the world population can perform second addition using a calculating machine?* We should not be surprised if the answer to our first question is not 100%. The United Nations' data show that answers to our second and third questions are not 100% [UNL13].

Analyzing further in the same direction, there are many more questions to be asked including: *How long did it take for us to recognize real world objects? How long did it take for us to take instructions (both in the form of signs and spoken languages) from elders and perform an addition task for the first time in our lives? How long did it take for us to recognize written alphabets and numerals? How long did it take for us to perform a written addition? How long did it take for human kind to be in this state of mind, which allows one to instruct and another to follow instructions and perform actions?* These questions might look a bit overwhelming and unnecessary at first, but these and many other similar questions govern our learning life cycles.

Now, let's take a slightly different example to set the stage for our Scala lessons. This too might look counterintuitive initially, but we will write a Scala program for this later in this chapter. Table 1.1 shows a biological categorization of human, dog, domestic pigeon, and cat. Here are some of the questions: *Is it a computational*

© Springer International Publishing AG 2017
B.P. Upadhyaya, *Programming with Scala*, Undergraduate
Topics in Computer Science, https://doi.org/10.1007/978-3-319-69368-2_1

problem? Do we have sufficient information to decide whether it is a computational problem?

Table 1.1: Sample Biological Taxonomy Data

SN	Hierarchy	Human	Dog	Domestic Pigeon	Cat
1	*Kingdom*	Animalia	Animalia	Animalia	Animalia
2	*Phylum*	Chordata	Chordata	Chordata	Chordata
3	*Class*	Mammalia	Mammalia	Aves	Mammalia
4	*Order*	Primates	Carnivora	Columbiformes	Carnivora
5	*Family*	Hominidae	Canidae	Columbidae	Felidae
6	*Genus*	Homo	Canis	Columba	Felis
7	*Species*	H. Sapiens	C. lupus	C. livia	F. catus

Let's say we are asked to build a dictionary or an information base that can be referred to to get information. Now, it is fairly convenient to decide whether it is a computational problem, if we have a computing background. But this might still be confusing if we do not have any idea about computing, because computation cannot be seen on the surface. Even Google search may not look like a computational problem on the surface, as we can't see any regular calculations. In fact, Google search is a complex computation.

Assume we don't have any knowledge of computing as defined by the OED. Probably it is fair to say that all the human beings search for at least one item in their lives. When we are searching for something, our mind performs computation. We might need to locate, count, or categorize items. Locating something might involve counting. For example, if we have to locate a book in another room, then we have to cross at least one door, assuming these are regular rooms in a regular house. Since we have enormous practice of going from one room to another room in our lives, we might be performing the computation even without realizing it. Now, let's think about what it takes to train an infant, as he/she grows, to perform the same task. Does the infant need to learn how to count in order to perform this task? Probably the answer is yes. And it might take years to train the infant. Learning computing is not much different from this infant's training. The major difference is age, along with accumulated knowledge. And of course, infants too can start learning computing these days.

We know how hard it is to live our lives without using any tools. Even in the stone age, our ancestors used some sort of tools: a stone, a stick, or slightly more sophisticated tools. Now, we all know why we need tools. Also we know that the same tool cannot be utilized to solve every problem in our lives. This is true in the case of computational tools as well. Since this book deals with a particular programming language, Scala, in details, let's be concrete and say that this is true for programming languages as well. Programming languages are a type of computational tool.

Now we have some ideas about computation. Let's ask another question: *Can every computational problem be computed?* Well, there are several university level courses dedicated to answer this question. For now, we focus on our two problems—addition and our tiny information base for biological taxonomy. The first one can certainly be computed. We limited the scope of the second problem and made it viable for computing. Please note that we did not go for genomics, which requires enormous computing power.

In the next section, we will discuss the basics of computing tools, called computers.

1.1 Introduction to Computers

Computers are tools that we can use to perform some computations and they come in various shapes and sizes. There are hundreds of companies around the world that manufacture varieties of computers and computer parts. Generally, a computationally useful computer has two categories of components—hardware and software. Hardware consumes energy and performs computations, whereas software contains the logic for operations. It is the software that instructs the hardware in order to achieve a computational goal. A computational goal can be as primitive as inverting a digit, i. e., converting 0 to 1 and vice-versa. In this book, we will learn a programming language that helps us to instruct computers, in order to achieve one or more computational goals. Clearly it is a software component that helps us to create other software components.

1.1.1 Basic Components

Digital computers have the following basic components:

- Memory Unit
- Processing Unit
- Storage Unit
- Input Device
- Output Device

Almost every digital computing machine has some sort of memory. For example, if we are performing the addition mentioned earlier, $1 + 1 = 2$, using a digital calculator, it remembers at least three different items: digit 1 (first operand), operation + (operator), and digit 1 (second operand). A typical laptop, say a laptop from *One Laptop per Child*, has much more memory than a typical calculator [OLC17]. The reason is that a laptop has to hold much more information and has to perform much more sophisticated operations than a typical calculator. And things might be different if we are referring to a scientific calculator. For now, we stick with a simple calculator that performs addition, subtraction, multiplication, and division.

In the case of our calculator, we need a unit that performs the addition operation. The unit that performs this kind of operation is called a *Processing Unit*. In the case of digital computers, every high level operation or computational goal like opening a file or googling a word is eventually represented with 1s and 0s; these are the only two signals a digital computer understands. Interestingly, this transformation is a complex process and is studied as a computer engineering degree in traditional universities. From this course's perspective, let's remember the fact that every program we write will be eventually processed by a processing unit. A common terminology used for such a processing unit is *Central Processing Unit* as there are other processing units in a typical computer. For example, a keyboard has a processor to process keyboard inputs.

Generally the term storage unit refers to permanent storage devices; these devices can retain data even after the power is switched off. Large files or data go to storage devices and are fetched to memory as per computational needs. Storage devices can be a small stick like a flash drive, or a hard drive like in a laptop or in a desktop, or an array of disks. In case of cloud computing, storage can be as big as hundreds of data centers around the world.

There are different ways to provide data to a computational device. Typing, speaking, and touching are common methods to provide input. Also different types of sensors can be utilized to provide input data. For example, a wind direction sensor can generate and supply data to a computational device. If we we are typing, a keyboard is a common way to provide input. Keys are continuously scanned for possible input. Microphones are common devices to capture voice signals. These analog signals are then converted to digital equivalents and fed to a computer. Please note that an analog to digital converter itself does some sort of computation, in addition to signal conversion. So in a typical computer, there are numerous processing units, commonly called processors. For touch related input, a digital keyboard can be available; in some cases, it could just be a swipe.

Output devices present the results of computations. Most often these results are visual and hence display devices are common output devices. Like computers, display devices can come in various shapes and sizes. Some displays are boxed together with central processing units, while others are packaged separately. Increasingly, display devices have been using liquid crystal display (LCD) technology. LCD makes displays much lighter compared with older popular technology like cathode ray tube (CRT).

1.1.2 Operation

Computers operate in different modes as far as program execution is concerned. A program is a set of instructions, written in computer understandable form, and mapped to one or more computation goals. If we are using portable computers, like laptops, most often the computation will be in real time, unless we instruct the machine to perform differently. But for large farm of computers and processes, the mode of operation can be batch processing.

Batch mode is an operating mode which takes set of operations and executes them in a non-real-time fashion. Also the results are often returned to the owner in a batch mode. This kind of operation is very common where there is massive data and real time processing is not feasible. For example, petabytes of data are generated from Facebook and if we need to infer something based on this large volume of data, real time processing based on state of the art computing technology is not practical. So, there is a clear need for a different mode of operation. Similarly, if certain high speed computing resources are in demand, we might need to provide time slots to each requester. This mode of operation is called time sharing. In fact, batch mode of operation might utilize time sharing.

1.2 Operating Systems

An operating system (OS), as the name suggests, is the software that operates hardware components. In order for us to execute our programs, we need an operating system. Our programs will be some of the software pieces that an operating system runs. Also if we need to access a service offered by an I/O device then we have to request the operating system for that service. One can think of the operating system as an administrator of the hardware resources. The operating system talks to various hardware components through drivers. Drivers are software programs that can process signals to and from hardware components.

A computer that is generally used by one person is called a personal computer (PC). PCs have the following popular operating systems:

- Linux family
- Mac OS family
- Windows family

Linux is the only open source operating system among the above three. Also it is the most popular. There are many dialects of Linux including Ubuntu, Suse, and Fedora core. In the early days Linux was difficult to install and manage. But now it is very different and Linux is as convenient as the Windows operating system. Most of websites, these days, are hosted in a server that runs Linux operating system. Linux was inspired by the Unix operating system, a popular enterprise operating system before Linux.

Mac OS is the operating system for Macintosh computers by Apple. Apple personal computers are known for their reliability and for their aesthetic value. Steve Jobs, one of the founders of Apple, talks about taste in computing and claims that Apple products provide good taste of computing. Remember we discussed computing and computation as defined in the OED, and now we are discussing taste in computing. It should be noted that programming languages are developed in that fashion too. Like Linux, Mac OS has its roots in Unix and if we know about one of these three, working with other two is fairly convenient.

Generally Windows is regarded as an easy operating system. It is a common operating system for personal computing devices. Some of hardware manufacturers have contracts with Microsoft, the company behind Windows, that allow them to sell Windows along with new hardware devices. For example, if we buy an IBM ThinkPad, now a Lenovo ThinkPad, we are most likely to get a Windows OS.

1.3 Programming Languages

Now we are getting closer to what we will be learning in this book. Programming languages can be categorized into two main categories:

- Low Level Programming Languages: Machine, Assembly
- High Level Programming Languages: Pascal, C, Java, Scala

Early digital computers involved relay based switching in order to carry out a typical computation. This means programming in 1s and 0s. The next level of programming was assembly language. Assembly language uses mnemonics; programs become longer and harder to comprehend.

```
...
mov dx, 3a8h
xor al, al
out dx, al
inc dx
mov cx, 256
xor al, al
...
```

Fig. 1.1: Sample Assembly Language Code Snippet

The code listing in Figure 1.1 has register level operations. A register is one of the smallest data holding places in a computer. The width of its registers partially determines the computational capacity of a computer. Computational capacity is often related to the speed of a computer. So assembly language programming means register level programming, which some programmers find interesting. It gives more power, as a programmer can directly access the content of a register. With this power comes a lot of responsibility on the programmer's side.

The programmer has to take care of fine grained computational details. For example, if a programmer is writing a program to subtract one number from another, and if these numbers do not fit to the width of one register, then it is the programmer's responsibility to store and manage each digit of those numbers. While performing subtraction, the programmer is required to take care of carry overs as well. This was the life of a programmer before high level programming languages were created.

mov, *xor*, *out*, and *inc* are called mnemonics and these provide a way to instruct a machine. Sometimes these are also known as machine instructions although there can be significant differences between these mnemonics and the machine instruction set of a particular microprocessor architecture. Generally, machine instruction sets are different for different microprocessor architecture, which means programs written for one architecture are not compatible with another architecture.

Now, we present a program to print "Welcome to programming" in each of the four different programming languages—Pascal, C, Java, and Scala. This will give us some idea on how programming languages have evolved in the history of computer science.

```
PROGRAM sampleprogram;
BEGIN
  writeln('Welcome to programming');
END.
```

Fig. 1.2: Sample Pascal Program

Figure 1.2 shows a code snippet for a Pascal program that prints "Welcome to programming" on the screen. The program starts with the keyword *PROGRAM*, which is followed by a program name; program name can be any valid identifier. The code to print the message on the screen is placed between two keywords– *BEGIN* and *END*. In fact, *writeln* is a procedure that takes a string, in this case, and outputs it to the screen, the output device. Please note that this procedure utilizes an output device. Just to remind ourselves, the way to handle an output device is through the operating system, which runs this Pascal program. In the case of high level programming languages, this method of handling input and output devices is hidden from the programmers so they can focus on solving computational problems at hand. There are many online resources available if you want to compile and run this program.

```
#include<stdio.h>
main() {
  printf("Welcome to programming");
}
```

Fig. 1.3: Sample C Program

The program that can print "Welcome to programming" in C is shown in Figure 1.3. There are many similarities between a Pascal program and a C program. Both contain a function, though named differently, to enclose statements; both use output function to print on the screen. But the syntax looks different. In C, we need to define a main function and put statements in between curly brackets. Also it uses *printf* instead of *writeln*. Further, if we are using a library function, then we need to include that library file, normally a header file that contains that library function. In this program, the first line of code (LOC) does that. Once a header file is included, all the functions within that header file are available, for use in our program.

```
public class TestProgram {
  public static void main(String[] arguments) {
    System.out.println("Welcome to programming");
  }
}
```

Fig. 1.4: Sample Java Program

Now, let's try to achieve the same using a Java program. In fact, Java is the closest language to Scala; Scala programs are compiled to *.class* files. Figure 1.4 shows a Java program that prints "Welcome to programming" on the screen. Java syntax looks significantly different from C syntax. First of all, we need to create a class and then write a main method inside that class. We saw a main function in a C program and we are seeing a main method in a Java program. There is a relationship between the two languages, as Java language was influenced by C language. Java methods need an access modifier, so do Java classes. We have *public* visibility for both the *TestProgram* class and the *main* method inside it. *println* is a method from *PrintStream* class; *System* class contains a field, *out*, of type *PrintStream*. We are invoking *println* method of *out* object and passing our message "Welcome to programming." Since the field *out* is static in *System* class, we can call it as *System.out*.

```
object TestProgram {
  def main(arguments: Array[String]): Unit = {
    println("Welcome to programming")
  }
}
```

Fig. 1.5: Sample Scala Program

Finally, we now discuss our much awaited Scala program. Scala uses a singleton object, a class with a single instance, in order to run the main method. So instead of a class, we have an object *TestProgram* that contains the main method. There are syntactical differences between Java and Scala. Types are separated by a colon in Scala and come after identifiers. Java syntax requires types to be written before the identifiers. Also Scala uses new line as a separator, between two statements or expressions. If we want to use two expressions in the same line, then they should be separated by a semicolon.

Now, if we compare all four high level languages for which we wrote sample programs, then we find *main* in three of them—C, Java, and Scala. In C, it is called the main function. In Java and Scala, it is called the main method. In Java, it is a static method; the concept is the same in Scala, with slightly different arrangements. Scala recommends singleton objects for static methods. Singleton objects are classes with only one instance; the instance is created the first time it is used, on demand.

All four languages have some pre-defined words like *class*, *object*, *PROGRAM*, *BEGIN*, *END*, etc. Also it is relatively faster to comprehend code written in Pascal, C, Java, and Scala compared with the code written in assembly language. That's why these languages are called high level languages; high in the sense that they are close to natural languages, like English. If we look at longer programs written in Pascal, C, Java, and Scala, then we get a feeling that Scala is much more close to English, a natural language. Similarly, Java is closer to English than C. So the language advancements are moving away from machine dependencies and trying to be as close as possible to human spoken languages.

1.4 Introduction to Scala

Scala was designed by professor Martin Odersky, who is also a co-designer of Java Generics. Also Dr. Odersky implemented a reference Java compiler. He is an academician, who has significant industrial experience. This blend of experience has allowed him to create programming languages, which are intellectually challenging as well as of applied nature. He has done a great job of unifying the object oriented paradigm with the functional paradigm. If there is one programming language that brings functional programming seamlessly to large numbers of industrial software engineers, that is Scala.

Scala programs run on a Java Virtual Machine (JVM). This has multiple advantages. One of the advantages is that JVMs have been around for more than two decades and their tools have matured. Also there are millions of applications running on JVMs. Since Scala programs compile to intermediate code, called byte code, developers don't have to modify their programs for new types of machines. If a new type of machine appears in the market, the machine manufacturer writes JVM for that machine and the same Scala programs will run in the new machine architecture. This concept was pioneered by the Java programming language, which is also credited with defining software engineering. Scala takes it one step further by seamlessly integrating functional programming with object oriented programming. Also Scala is a purely object oriented programming language. Further, recent advancements in Java were inspired by Scala.

With that short introduction, now let's write programs for the computational problems that we introduced in the beginning of this chapter. Figure 1.6 shows a Scala program that defines two numbers to be added, adds the numbers, and then prints the sum on the screen. The first line starting with *package* provides the package name; a Scala package is pretty much like a package in daily life, in the sense that it is a name space to house classes, objects, traits, etc., that collectively achieve one or more computation goals.

```
package com.equalinformation.scala.programs
object AddTwoIntegers {
    def main(arguments: Array[String]): Unit = {
        val firstNumber = 1
        val secondNumber = 1
        val sum = firstNumber + secondNumber
        println("The sum is "+sum)
    }
}
```

Fig. 1.6: Program to Add Two Pre-defined Numbers

Now, if we want to perform addition for another set, 13 and 29, that we presented earlier in this chapter, then we need to replace the two 1s by 13 and 29. The order does not matter as addition is commutative. Once we replace the two operands and re-run the program, we get the sum, 42, printed on the screen. This implementation is too specific as operands are hard coded; every time we need to compute addition of two numbers, we have to replace the two operands. Now, we can improve this program by making it a bit more generic. In order to make it generic, we modify the program so that it takes two integers from a keyboard. So every time we need to compute addition, we just need to run the program and input two integers from the keyboard. In this way, we don't have to modify the program and re-compile.

```
package com.equalinformation.scala.programs
import scala.io.StdIn._
object AddTwoIntegers {
    def main(arguments: Array[String]): Unit = {
        print("Enter the first integer: ")
        val firstNumber = readInt()
        print("Enter the second integer: ")
        val secondNumber = readInt()
        val sum = firstNumber + secondNumber
        println("The sum is "+sum)
    }
}
```

Fig. 1.7: Program to Add Two Numbers

Figure 1.7 presents the improved version. We use *readInt()* method to read an integer from the keyboard. Since this method is available in *StdIn* object, which is packaged in *scala.io* package, we have the import statement, *import scala.io.StdIn._*. The underscore, '_', at the end of the import directs the compiler to import everything in the object *StdIn*. Note that we have re-used many LOCs from our previous program. Re-usability is one of the desirable attributes of computer programs; this is certainly true for Scala programs. Please note that while generalizing the program we did not write everything from scratch; we made the least modification to meet the new requirements. The requirement change in this case was to read operands from keyboard, instead of hard coding in our program.

Now let's write a Scala program to solve the second computational problem that we discussed in the beginning of this chapter. Figure 1.8 shows the implementation for data presented in Table 1.1. Ideally, data comes from some persistence systems. Since this volume is about Scala language exploration, we will make all the programs self-contained in terms of data.

```scala
package com.equalinformation.scala.programs
object BioTaxonomy {
  def main(args: Array[String]): Unit = {
    val humanTaxonomy = Map("Kingdom" -> "Animalia",
                            "Phylum" -> "Chordata",
                            "Class" -> "Mammalia",
                            "Order" -> "Primates",
                            "Family" -> "Hominidae",
                            "Genus" -> "Homo",
                            "Species" -> "H. Sapiens")
    val dogTaxonomy = Map("Kingdom" -> "Animalia",
                          "Phylum" -> "Chordata",
                          "Class" -> "Mammalia",
                          "Order" -> "Carnivora",
                          "Family" -> "Canidae",
                          "Genus" -> "Canis",
                          "Species" -> "C. lupus" )
    val pigeonTaxonomy = Map("Kingdom" -> "Animalia",
                             "Phylum" -> "Chordata",
                             "Class" -> "Aves",
                             "Order" -> "Columbiformes",
                             "Family" -> "Columbidae",
                             "Genus" -> "Columba",
                             "Species" -> "C. livia")
    val catTaxonomy = Map("Kingdom" -> "Animalia",
                          "Phylum" -> "Chordata",
                          "Class" -> "Mammalia",
                          "Order" -> "Carnivora",
                          "Family" -> "Felidae",
                          "Genus" -> "Felis",
                          "Species" -> "F. catus")
    val taxonomyList = List(humanTaxonomy, dogTaxonomy,
      pigeonTaxonomy, catTaxonomy)
    var count = 0;
    taxonomyList.foreach(_.values.foreach(x => x match {
      case "Felis" => count += 1
      case _ => count += 0
    }))
    println("Total cat taxonomy found: "+count)
  }
}
```

Fig. 1.8: Program for Biological Taxonomy Information Base

Figure 1.8 implements an information base for the data presented in Table 1.1. Each category is first represented as a Map; the representation should be fairly obvious to read. We will discuss syntactical details later in other chapters. The program then creates a list that contains all the maps; this is to create holistic data so that we can perform a search by referring to one data structure. The LOC that contains embedded *foreach* navigates all the values in the *taxonomyList*. We use pattern matching to find the occurrence of *Felis*, which helps us to conclude the availability of taxonomy information for the cat family. We will discuss pattern matching in detail in Chapter 10.

1.5 Program Attributes

We saw several programs in earlier sections. When we embark on a professional programming career, there are certain attributes that fellow professionals would like to see in our programs. These program attributes not only make projects more successful but also help us foster our professional relationships, which create positive dynamics for the team as well as for the community that we become part of. The following attributes are most common in industrial software engineering.

- Comprehensible
- Maintainable
- General
- Simple
- Modular
- Efficient
- Correct and accurate

Programs that are faster to read are said to have better or higher *readability*. A program that we write today might look strange in about six months and hence it is important to write readable programs so that they are easy to maintain in the future. Generally, software applications last more than a year and it is also true that team members change over a period of time for various reasons. In this context, programs that are comprehensible are much more desirable. This is one of the reason why engineers and scientists came up with high level programming languages. High level programming languages allow us to write much more readable programs compared with assembly languages.

The maintainability of a program is closely related to its readability. A program that has higher readability is easier to maintain. Many development teams recommend using a meaningful identifier instead of just a single letter. Also adding comments helps to understand the program better. Package naming, packages organization, configuration organization, etc. help to improve the maintenance of a code base.

In Section 1.4, we saw an example of making a program generic. Generic programs can cover more computational cases than a specific program. Of course, in some cases, programs have to be specific, in order to provide better value. This decision has to be made based on who is buying the software. If customers need specific programs, then we deliver them. But as a general principle, generic programs are more useful, in the sense that they cover larger computational cases.

A computational problem can have multiple programming solutions. Simpler solutions are cost effective to maintain. In a typical software application life cycle, maintenance consumes more resources than original development. It is also our observation that people have different attitudes toward simplicity in different dynamics. But in the long run, simplicity certainly pays off.

For large and complex programs, it is very important to organize the code so that navigation becomes faster. Also it is a common practice to group programs based on their functionality. In this way, if something has to be fixed for a particular functionality, then the developers know which module to look at. In a typical industrial software application, there can be hundreds of classes. Modularity can be implemented in different flavors. Writing several services and providing an interface to those services, is an example of making code modular. Sometimes, modularity can also be achieved by packaging. In fact, closely related services are packaged together.

Efficiency is equally important. A program should be able to provide a computational service by consuming minimum memory and minimum processing power. When we design a program or collection of programs, it is important to keep efficiency in mind, as infinite computational power is not available. Even if infinite computational power was available, we need to achieve our computational goals in a finite amount of time, relative to human life. So time is another factor to consider for efficiency.

Correctness indicates whether a solution satisfies requirements; generally, accuracy means precision. An accurate solution may not be correct. For example, we can get a solution that is accurate to the fifth decimal place with the incorrect formula. On the other hand, we can have the right formula and the wrong types, and get unintentional rounding of decimal places. One of the things to keep in mind as a programmer is the selection of the right data types and the right programming constructs, which produce accurate results. Correctness might go beyond programming constructs, including the right algorithms and the right formulae.

1.6 Conclusion

In this chapter, we discussed introductory computing concepts, including widely used terminologies—computing and computation. Then we discussed the tool aspect of computing by introducing computer components. In a typical modern digital computer, we find a memory unit to hold run time information, a processing unit to do processing, a storage unit for persistence, input devices to provide input, and output devices to send output to. Every computer needs a software system to operate it, called the operating system. We briefly discussed three most popular operating systems—Linux, Mac OS, and Windows.

Next, we discussed programming languages. Programming languages can be divided into two main categories—low level and high level. Machine code and assembly language are low level programming languages. Generally, low level programming refers to programming that uses either machine code or mnemonics; mnemonics map to machine instruction sets. Scala, Java, C, and Pascal are high level programming languages; high level programming languages are closer to natural languages and use words from natural languages. Programs written in high level programming languages are much easier to comprehend, compared with programs written in assembly languages. Next, we introduced the topic of this book, the Scala programming language. Then we provided solutions to two computational problems discussed in the beginning of this chapter. Finally, we discussed elements of a good program. In Chapter 2, we will learn Scala fundamentals.

1.7 Review Questions

1. What is a difference between computation and computing?
2. List the basic components of a typical modern digital computer.
3. What roles do operating systems play?
4. List the three most popular operating systems today.
5. Why is low level programming not efficient in terms of program development?
6. Name at least five high level programming languages.
7. Write three differences between Scala and Java.
8. What is the philosophy behind Scala?
9. Is functional programming better than object oriented programming?
10. What are some of the attributes of a good computer program?
11. Where can we find Scala installation information?

1.8 Problems

1. Write a program to print "Scala is fun." on the screen.
2. Write a program to calculate the difference between two integers. *Pre-condition*: The two integers should be read from a keyboard. *Post-condition*: The difference should be displayed on the screen.
3. Write a program to print each letter of a string. *Pre-condition*: The string should be read from a keyboard. *Post-condition*: Each letter should be printed on a separate line.

1.9 Answers to Review Questions

1. According to the *Oxford English Dictionary*, the word computation refers to mathematical calculation and computing refers to the use of computing machines in order to perform computation.
2. The basic components of a typical modern computers are:

   • Memory Unit
   • Processing Unit
   • Storage Unit
   • Input Device
   • Output Device

3. Operating systems administer the hardware. In other words, operating systems give life to the hardware. Also operating systems act as a mediator between hardware and application software.
4. The three most popular operating systems today are Linux, Mac OS, and Windows.
5. Low level programming languages require developers to program at register level. Further, developers need to take care of fine grained details. Also the use of mnemonics is not as comprehensible as natural language based words.
6. Five high level programming languages are Scala, Java, Go, Swift, and Python.
7. The three differences between Scala and Java are:

   • Scala is a purely object oriented language but Java is not.
   • Scala was designed with the aim of combining the object oriented paradigm with the functional paradigm but Java was designed to be an object oriented language. Over the course of time, Java has adopted some functional programming features.
   • Scala had built-in features for program parallelism from the beginning but Java introduced it much later.

8. The Scala designer, Dr. Martin Odersky, believes that the object oriented paradigm can be combined with the functional paradigm to provide a better computing experience. And he has proven it.
9. It depends on the nature of the computational problem. So there is no definite answer. For some problems, the object oriented approach might be better, for other problems the functional approach might work better. Further, there can be problems that can benefit from a combination of these two programming paradigms.
10. Some of the attributes of a good computer program are:

    • Readable
    • General enough to cover wider computational problem space
    • Maintainable
    • Simple
    • Modular
    • Efficient in term of memory and CPU

11. Scala installation information can be found at `https://www.scala-lang.org/`

1.10 Solutions to Problems

1.
```scala
object SolutionToProblem1 {
  def main(arguments: Array[String]): Unit = {
    println("Scala is fun.")
  }
}
```

2.
```scala
import scala.io.StdIn._
object SolutionToProblem2 {
  def main(arguments: Array[String]): Unit = {
    print("Enter the first integer: ")
    val firstNumber = readInt()
    print("Enter the second integer: ")
    val secondNumber = readInt()
    val difference = firstNumber - secondNumber
    println("The difference is "+difference)
  }
}
```

3.
```scala
object SolutionToProblem3 {
  def main(arguments: Array[String]): Unit = {
    print("Please enter a string: ")
    val inputString = scala.io.StdIn.readLine()
    inputString.toString.foreach(println)
  }
}
```

Chapter 2
Scala Fundamentals

In this chapter, we will cover building blocks of the Scala programming language. As name suggests, building blocks are like alphabets of a programming language. One of the observations we made both in industry as well as in academia is that learners tend to overlook basic building blocks, thinking that the subject matter is too basic. This creates a knowledge gap and when these building blocks are combined with complex algorithms, the combination looks harder to comprehend and requires learners to come back and learn the building blocks again. To avoid this, you should try to learn the building blocks well at the first attempt by paying attention. In isolation, building blocks look simple.

2.1 Literals

We use literals to create programs. They are directly or indirectly connected with natural languages and how we perform computations. For example, *String* is a collection of characters. But it turns out that we need individual characters as well. From a machine's point of view, this categorization helps to allocate memory efficiently.

2.1.1 Character Literals

Have you ever noticed the use of a single character in your daily life? Most probably the answer is yes. It might be for tagging items, it might be for enumerating items, etc. Well, it could equally be your grades. Scala allows us to express a single character using a character literal. A character literal can be defined by enclosing a single character in quotes. It can be either a printable unicode character or an escape sequence, defined in Section 2.1.6.
Valid characters:

© Springer International Publishing AG 2017
B.P. Upadhyaya, *Programming with Scala*, Undergraduate
Topics in Computer Science, https://doi.org/10.1007/978-3-319-69368-2_2

`'a'`   `'\u0061'`   `'\t'`   `'\n'`

Sample declaration:

```
val b:Char = 'b'
```

The first one is character *a* and the second one is also character *a*, because unicode *0061* is for letter *a*. The last two characters print tab and new line, respectively. Please note the quotes: unlike how it is printed here, you have to use the same single quote, on both sides, when you type the code.

2.1.2 String Literals

Whether we are reading a newspaper on-line or reading a book, we use text extensively. Scala facilitates textual representation with string literals. A string is a sequence of characters. A string literal can be defined by enclosing a sequence of characters in double quotes. The characters can be either printable unicode characters or escape sequences, defined in Section 2.1.6.
Valid strings:

```
"Welcome"     "Welcome\tto\tprogramming"
"Scala is fun"
"\"Scala\" supports functional programming"

""" This is an example
of multi-line
string literals. """
```

Sample declaration:

```
val c:String = "Scala"
```

The second string literal above has a tab character in between words and hence the output is *Welcome to programming*, with spacing between words equal to the tab width. If we need double quotes, then these should be escaped, as shown in the fourth string literal. The output of the fourth string literal is *"Scala" supports functional programming*. The last string literal is an example of a multi-line string and it should be enclosed by three consecutive double quotes.

We can perform a rich set of operations on a string. For example, *reverse* reverses a given string: *"this".reverse* prints *siht*. In order to split a sentence into words *split* can be used: *"Scala is powerful".split(" ")* prints *Array[String] = Array(Scala, is, powerful)*. Similarly, a word in a string can be replaced by using *replace*: *"Scala is powerful".replace("powerful", "fun")* results *Scala is fun*.

2.1.3 Integer Literals

We use whole numbers a lot in our daily lives. We can express these numbers using Scala integer literals. Integer literals are widely used and are of two types based on length—Int or Long. Long integers are expressed with a suffix l or L. For example, 25 is an integer and 25L is a long integer. The permitted values for type Int are from -2^{31} to $2^{31} - 1$, inclusive. Auto conversion happens for small type: Byte, Short, and Char. When a type falls within the range of a smaller type, the number is converted to that smaller type along with the type information. Table 2.1 presents integer types and corresponding ranges.

Table 2.1: Integer Literals and Ranges

Type	Range
Byte	-2^7 to $2^7 - 1$
Short	-2^{15} to $2^{15} - 1$
Char	0 to $2^{16} - 1$
Int	-2^{31} to $2^{31} - 1$

Valid integers:

```
5 -5 0 25 0xAF
```

Sample declaration:

```
val a:Int = 5
```

Invalid declaration:

```
val d:Int = 3999999999
```

It is invalid, because the value assigned is out of integer range, as discussed above.

2.1.4 Floating Point Literals

In mathematics, we use real numbers frequently. Scala allows us to express those real numbers with the help of floating point numbers, called floating point literals. Floating point literals cover Float as well as Double. Float covers all IEEE 754 32-bit single-precision binary floating point values and Double covers all IEEE 754 64-bit double-precision binary floating point values. Float types have optional suffixes: f, F, d, or D.
Valid floating point numbers:

```
1e10f 1e-10f 5.5  .5
```

Sample declaration:

```
val a = 1e-10f
```

Invalid declaration:

```
val a:Int = 1e-10f
```

It is invalid, because the value on the right hand side is not an integer value. The right data type, in this case, is Float.

2.1.5 Boolean Literals

We need a way to express yes or no, equivalently true or false. In our daily lives, we do that quite a lot. Similarly, Scala has a feature called boolean literal, which allows us to express yes and no.
Valid boolean values:

```
true false
```

Sample declarations:

```
val a = true
val b: Boolean = false
```

2.1.6 Escape Sequences

Escape sequences can be used to print special characters. The following escape sequences can be used with character and string literals.

```
\b      \u0008 Back space (BS)
\t      \u0009 Horizontal tab (HT)
\n      \u000a Line feed (LF)
\f      \u000c Form feed (FF)
\r      \u000d Carriage return (CR)
\"      \u0022 Double quote (")
'       \u0027 Single quote (')
\\      \u005c Back slash (\)
```

So when the statement *print("a\nb")* is executed, characters a and b are printed in separate lines. First, character a is printed, then new line character is printed, which causes b to be printed in a separate line.

2.1.7 Symbol Literals

Symbol is a case class. We will discuss classes in Chapter 3. A symbol 'y is a shortcut for the expression *scala.Symbol("y")*. *Symbol* is a case class and can be found in package *scala*, with the following definition.

```
package scala
final case class Symbol private (name: String) {
    override def toString: String = "'" + name
}
```

Figure 2.1 shows a typical identifier comparison with *eq* operator (or method). The output is *true*. A string comparison may involve character to character comparison, in some cases, and hence lookups tend to be more efficient with symbol literals, as *eq* can be applied. Comparisons, with symbol literals, are constant time (i.e. O(1)).

Fig. 2.1: Symbol literals

```
object Literals {
    def main(args: Array[String]): Unit = {
        val a ='sampleIdentifier
        println("sampleIdentifier" eq a.name)
    }
}
```

2.1.8 Other Lexical Elements

1. Whitespace and Comments
   In English, words are separated by a space, approximately equivalent to the width of one character. Similarly, in Scala, tokens are separated by a whitespace; tokens can also be separated by comments. Scala has two types of comments—single line and multi-line. Single line comments start with // and extend to the end of line. Multi-line comments are embedded within /* and */. It is a good practice to comment our code. See the code fragment below.

```
...
// Length
val a = 5
// Breadth
val b = 4
val area = a * b
...
```

The code is certainly more comprehensible, with the help of comments; maintenance becomes a lot easier, specially when the program is to be maintained by a different person. Similarly, let's look at the multi-line comment below.

```
...
/*
 This program calculates an area
 of a rectangle.
*/
val length = 5
val breadth = 4
val area = length * breadth
...
```

The code fragment above demonstrates a multi-line comment. Comparing this comment with the previous comment should give you an idea of when to use each of them. Please also note the identifier names in these two code fragments.

2. Newline Characters

Statements in Scala can be terminated by semicolons or newlines. In other words, semicolons are optional, if we use newlines as separators, and newlines are optional, if we use semicolons as separators. Let's look at the four code fragments below.

```
...
val side = 5
val area = side * side
...
```

```
...
val side = 5;
val area = side * side;
...
```

```
...
val side = 5; val area = side * side;
...
```

```
...
val side = 5; val area = side * side
println(area)
...
```

All of the above four code fragments are syntactically correct. You can follow the approach that best suits you, if you have the liberty to decide. If you are working in a team environment, it is good to have common conventions.

2.2 Identifiers and Reserved Words

Think of a quadratic equation of the form $ax^2 + bx + c = 0$. x is a variable and a, b, and c are constants. All of these are identifiers; they identify or represent values. It is important to remember that there are rules that govern what kind of values they hold, including whether they can hold multiple values. Also please recall the introductory concepts from Chapter 1. We are discussing elements of a typical computing environment. Our thought processes should be geared toward how we can organize the computing elements so that we can achieve our computational goals.

Similarly, an identifier in Scala denotes a computational element. A computational element can be an integer, a string, a character, a class, etc. An identifier can start with a letter and the starting letter can be followed by any arbitrary sequence of letters, digits, or underscore. The '$' character should not be used to define identifiers as it is reserved for compiler-generated identifiers. Reserved words are predefined words that cannot be used as identifiers. Table 2.2 presents reserved words in Scala.

Table 2.2: Reserved Words

abstract	case	catch	class	def
do	else	extends	false	final
finally	for	forSome	if	implicit
import	lazy	match	new	null
object	override	package	private	protected
return	sealed	super	this	throw
trait	try	true	type	val
var	while	with	yield	
_	:=	=> <-	<: <%	>: # @

Valid identifiers:

```
length    _y    +    _MIN    green_?
```

2.3 Types

From a user's perspective, types are categories that have common properties. For example, *Int* and *Long* are both integers. From our arithmetic knowledge, we know that all integers have some common properties that can be leveraged for a computational goal. For example, when we add two integers, digit by digit, there is something called carry, which is added to the next higher position digit.

Scala has many fundamental types, which can be used as building blocks for custom defined types. *Byte, Short, Int, Long, Char* are some of the basic types. *Float* and *Double* are types to represent decimal numbers. All of these types together are called *numeric types*. The type *String* is used to represent text; it is part of *java.lang* package. All other types described here are part of *scala* package.

```
object TypesDemo {
    def main(args: Array[String]): Unit = {
        val length: Int = 5
        val breadth = 2.5
        val area = length * breadth
        println(area)
        val problemName: String = "Area of a rectangle"
        val purpose = "Practice"
        println(purpose+": "+problemName)
    }
}
```

Fig. 2.2: Types Demonstration

Figure 2.2 shows three different type declarations—Int, Float, and String. Please note that *length* is explicitly declared as *Int* but the type for *breadth* comes from type inference. This is one of the advantages of programming in Scala; it has the capability to infer type based on the corresponding value. So *breadth* gets type *Float* and subsequently the type of the area is inferred as *Float*, because when an integer is multiplied with a floating point number, the result is a floating point number.

In the case of Scala, when an *Int* is multiplied with a *Float*, the resultant type is *Float*. Similarly, the first string, *problemName*, is declared explicitly, whereas the type for second string, *purpose*, is derived from its value. The output for the second *println* is the concatenation of three strings, the second one being the value within double quotes. The output for the first *println* is 12.5.

2.4 Declarations and Definitions

A declaration is a way to tell the Scala compiler about names, types, parameters, etc. Using definitions, we can provide detail information including values and steps for computation. A value declaration takes the form *val x: T*; a value definition takes the form *val x: T = e*, where *val* is a reserved word to tell the compiler that the corresponding identifier is an immutable value, which means it cannot be changed later; *x* is an identifier; *T* is a type, and *e* is an expression. So *x* gets a value, which is a result of evaluation of the expression *e*. When we explicitly specify the type *T*, the result of evaluation of expression *e* should be *T*, otherwise it is a compile time error.

Figure 2.3 shows value declarations as well as definitions. This program has four values: *itemName*, *quantity*, *priceInDollar*, and *totalPrice*. Scala's values are constants, which means re-assignment is a compile time error. The first three identifiers

```
object DeclarationsDefinitionsDemo {
   def main(args: Array[String]): Unit = {
      val itemName = "Orange"
      val quantity = 5
      val priceInDollar = 2
      val totalPrice: Int = quantity * priceInDollar
      println("Total price of "+itemName+" = "+totalPrice)
   }
}
```

Fig. 2.3: Value Declaration and Definition

get their type through Scala's type inference, whereas the fourth one is explicitly declared. Declaration and definition are done within the same line of code. The last line of code performs auto conversion of integer values to corresponding string values. If we have + in between string and numeric values, the numeric values are automatically converted to string values and then concatenated.

A variable declaration has the form *var x: T*; a variable definition takes the form *var x: T = e*. The main difference between *val* and *var* is that *var* can be re-assigned a value. *A very important thing to note is that* var *may not be safe for parallel programming. Sequential programs written using* val *are easier to transform to parallel programs.* So you are highly encouraged to program using *val* and avoid *var* whenever possible.

```
object VarDeclarationsDefinitionDemo {
   def main(args: Array[String]): Unit = {
      var itemName = "Orange"
      var quantity = 5
      var priceInDollar = 2
      var totalPrice = quantity * priceInDollar
      println(itemName+": "+totalPrice)
      itemName = "Apple"
      quantity = 6
      priceInDollar = 3
      totalPrice = quantity * priceInDollar
      println(itemName+": "+totalPrice)
   }
}
```

Fig. 2.4: Variable Declaration and Definition

Figure 2.4 shows variable declarations as well as variable definitions. Please note that all the variables have been re-used. First, we assign values for orange and calculate total price and print the value. Next, we use the same variables and assign values corresponding to apple and perform a similar calculation, which is followed by a *println* statement.

This is perfectly fine in a sequential execution. We will see later how to represent real world objects with Scala objects. Once we do that, there will be some getter and setter methods associated with each variable. If the setter methods are called from concurrent processes then the consistency becomes important. That's when we start realizing the importance of immutability.

Next, let's take a short example of type declaration. Figure 2.5 shows a type alias definition. *intList* can be used as *List[Int]*, which is exactly what is being done in the next LOC, *val a: intList = List(1,2,3)*. Here *a* gets its type from type alias, which in turn gets its type from its definition. So the list creation on the right hand side should comply with the type definition of type alias. If it doesn't, then it is a compile time error.

```
object TypeDeclarationDefinitionDemo {
    def main(args: Array[String]): Unit = {
        type intList = List[Int]
        val a: intList = List(1,2,3)
        a.foreach(println)
    }
}
```

Fig. 2.5: Type Definition

We will cover the remaining declarations and definitions in later chapters.

2.5 Expressions

Expressions can be evaluated and the result of evaluation can be assigned or returned to the caller. Also an expression has a type, which may come from Scala inference. If type is declared as in *val x: T = e*, then the type of *e* must match with *T*. The simplest expressions are literals. For example, in *val a = 5*, *val* is a reserved word, which directs the compiler that identifier *a* is value, = is an assignment operator, and *5* is a simple expression, an integer literal. In Scala, an expression can be any one of the following types:

1. Literal
2. The *null* value
3. Designator
4. *this* and *super*
5. Named and default argument
6. Method values
7. Tuples
8. Instance creation expression
9. Block

10. Typed expression
11. Annotated expression
12. Conditional expression
13. While loop expression
14. Do loop expression
15. For loop
16. Return expression
17. Throw expression
18. Try expression
19. Constant expression

We will discuss each of these expression types in the relevant chapters. For now, let's look at an example with several expressions. Figure 2.6 shows three different types of expression. The first one has digit *6* as an expression, which is a literal expression. The second one is *a + 1*. For this expression, type inference uses the type of *a*, Float, to determine the type of *b*. And of course, *a + 1* is evaluated and assigned to *b*.

```
object ExpressionsDemo {
    def main(args: Array[String]): Unit = {
        val a: Float = 6
        val b = a + 1
        println(b)
        val c = {
            val d = 2
            val e = 3
            d + e
        }
        println(c)
    }
}
```

Fig. 2.6: Expressions

The next expression is a block expression. Scala has an interesting feature that allows us to assign a block to an identifier and use it as a value. The block is evaluated and types are inferred before assigning value to the variable *c*. The type of *d* and *e* can be inferred based on their value on the right hand side, and *d + e* will have the same type, which is *Int*, in this case. Now, the last statement of the block is a return statement; Scala does not require us to write *return* explicitly. So the value of *d + e* is assigned to *c*, which is *5*. The first *println* prints *7.0* and the second *println* prints *5*.

2.6 Conclusion

In this chapter, we covered character literals, which are the most fundamental building blocks. Then we discussed string literals; these are widely used as text represents a large percentage of information processing. Similarly, we covered numerals and their range. Escape sequences are important literals to remember as these become a source of bugs if used improperly. Symbol literals are not widely used but these are faster to lookup. Comments are an important part of program documentation. Newline sounds obvious, but in Scala it has a special meaning, i.e., a newline eliminates the need for a semicolon.

2.7 Review Questions

1. What is the difference between 'a' and "a"?
2. Where does the type come from in *val languageName = "Scala"*?
3. What is the range of type *Int* in Scala?
4. Is *0xAD* a valid integer?
5. Is *0xBG* a valid integer?
6. Is *oxCF* a valid integer?
7. Is *val c: Int = 1e-20f* a valid declaration?
8. Is *val x = true* a valid declaration and a valid definition?
9. Is *val y: Boolean = 1* a valid definition?
10. How is a multi-line comment written?
11. Can a new line be used as a statement terminator?
12. Can a semicolon be used as a statement terminator?
13. When can't a semicolon be replaced by a new line for statement termination?
14. Is *forSome* a reserved word?
15. Why is a type important?
16. What is the simplest possible expression?

2.8 Problems

1. Write a program to reverse the letters of a word. Hint: you can use the Scala library.
2. Write a program to read two words from a keyboard, concatenate them, and then reverse the letters.
3. Write a program that uses a block to read length and breadth as double precision floating point numbers. This block also calculates the area and returns or assigns the result to a variable called *area*. Print the area on the console.

2.9 Answers to Review Questions

1. 'a' is a character literal and "a" is a string literal.
2. In *val languageName = "Scala"*, the type comes from inference.
3. The range of type *Int* is 2^{-31} to $2^{31} - 1$.
4. *0xAD* is a valid integer, it is in hexadecimal representation.
5. *0xBG* is not a valid integer, *G* is not part of hexadecimal representation.
6. *oxCF* is not a valid integer, it should start with *0x*, not *ox*.
7. *val c: Int = 1e-20f* is not a valid declaration, because the value on the right hand side is not an integer value.
8. *val x = true* is a valid declaration and definition, the type is inferred automatically.
9. *val y: Boolean = 1* is not a valid definition because *1* is not part of boolean literals.
10. A multi-line comment is embedded in /* */.
11. Yes, a new line can be used as a statement terminator.
12. Yes, a semicolon can be used as a statement terminator.
13. If there are two statements in a single line, the first one must be terminated by using a semicolon.
14. Yes, *forSome* is a Scala reserved word.
15. A type helps to categorize building blocks and makes it convenient to analyze a program. From the machine's perspective, types are used for memory allocation.
16. The simplest possible expression is a literal.

2.10 Solutions to Problems

1.
```scala
object ReverseLetters {
    def main(args: Array[String]) {
        print("Please enter a word: ")
        val word = scala.io.StdIn.readLine();
        val wordReversed = word.toString.reverse
        println(wordReversed)
    }
}
```

2.
```scala
import scala.io.StdIn._
object StringConcat {
  def main(args: Array[String]): Unit = {
    print("Please enter the first word: ")
    val firstWord = readLine()
    print("Please enter the second word: ")
    val secondWord = readLine()
    val combination = firstWord.toString.concat(
      secondWord.toString)
    println(combination)
    val wordCombreversed = combination.reverse
    println(wordCombreversed)
  }
}
```

3.
```scala
import scala.io.StdIn._
object AreaCalculation {
  def main(args: Array[String]): Unit = {
    val area = {
      print("Please enter the length: ")
      val length = readDouble()
      print("Please enter the breadth: ")
      val breadth = readDouble()
      length * breadth
    }
    println(area)
  }
}
```

Chapter 3
Classes and Objects

Classes and objects in Scala allow us to model real world classes and objects. Let's recall our education system. If you went through a formal education system anywhere in the world, most likely you went through a classification system, i. e., you joined in the first level, you learnt and changed your knowledge status, and then you were promoted to the next level. In some countries, these are known as class 1, class 2, ..., class 12. Whatever the naming convention, the idea is same, i.e., you are in a certain level of knowledge, you learn new things, your level changes, you are tested and then formally recognized.

What are the advantages of classification? In an education system, if two people are enrolled in the same level, you can safely assume that their knowledge level is close enough to be grouped together so that they benefit from common resources. Of course, sometimes there can be exceptions; we will have similar situations in Scala as well. Some examples of common resources are classrooms, teachers, teaching materials, etc. Also with this classification, teachers know how to handle students. If we look at traditional biological classification, we notice that animals with similar behavior and structure are put in the same category. What is the advantage? It is convenient to study and analyze. This is true in Scala as well. Remember our discussion in Chapter 1. We are using computers to solve real world problems.

By now, you have already seen several complete programs using objects. You might have developed some intuitions based on that. Now, we first discuss the building blocks of a class and an object, which set the stage for declarations as well as definitions.

3.1 Class Members

A class has two important members—field and method. A field can be a variable or a constant value, which is used to hold a value. This value represents a state of an object. A method is used to represent the behavior of a real world object. In other words, a method is used to process computational parameters.

© Springer International Publishing AG 2017
B.P. Upadhyaya, *Programming with Scala*, Undergraduate
Topics in Computer Science, https://doi.org/10.1007/978-3-319-69368-2_3

Let's take an example of a real world object and model it with Scala programs. Let's assume that we have a circular object with radius 5 and we need to calculate its area. In order to create a comprehensible solution, we need to create a class called *Circle*. Since radius is an attribute of a circle, we should have a field called *radius*. Also we are going to calculate the area, so we need a variable to hold its value. Let's call it *area*. So we have two fields for our *Circle* class.

Next, we need a method to compute area. Let's call it *computeArea*. This method uses the formula, $area = \pi r^2$, to calculate the area of a circle. The value of π is available as a constant in the object *Math*, in the Scala package *scala.math*, which forwards to *java.lang.Math*. Similarly, *pow* method is available in the same object.

```scala
class Circle {
    var radius = 0
    var area = 0.0
    def computeArea(): Unit = {
        area = Math.PI * Math.pow(radius,2)
    }
}

object CircleApplication {
    def main(args: Array[String]): Unit = {
        val circleObj = new Circle
        circleObj.radius = 5
        circleObj.computeArea()
        println(circleObj.area)
    }
}
```

Fig. 3.1: Circle Application

Figure 3.1 shows a complete solution to this problem. We have the *Circle* class described earlier and then we have a circle application called *CircleApplication*. The two variables in the *Circle* class require initialization. If we are expecting a floating point result then *area* should be initialized with a floating point value so that the type *Float* is assigned to the variable *area*. There is a single LOC in the method *computeArea*. Once the right hand side expression is evaluated, the result is assigned to *area*, which is a class variable.

The class *Circle* does not run by itself. In order to make use of it, we need to create an application. *CircleApplication* is a runnable application. We have seen similar examples before, but without a class. Here, we have modularized the code. Please remember that modularity is one of the attributes that we discussed in Chapter 1. Also the *Circle* class is re-usable.

The first LOC in the main method creates an object called *circleObj* of type *Circle*. Then the second LOC assigns value 5 to the field *radius*. The default access modifier for class members is public. Please also note that a getter method and a setter method are generated for each public variable in the class during compilation.

For now, let's remember that *<object-name>.<field-name>* gives access to a public field in a class; a method can be accessed in the same way and parentheses are optional if there are no parameters to pass. When we run this program, we should see the result 78.54 on the console.

3.2 Class Definitions

Classes are defined in terms of templates; this is true for objects as well. Here is the template definition from the Scala language specification:

```
TmplDef          ::= ['case'] 'class' ClassDef
                 |   ['case'] 'object' ObjectDef
                 |   'trait' TraitDef
```

It can optionally start with *case*, which should be followed by either *class* or *object* and then a corresponding definition. Alternatively, it can start with *trait*, which should be followed by a trait definition.

A class definition can start with *case*, which is for a case class. A case class is a model class; it has fields, which can be defined as constructor parameters. If it is a regular class, then it should start with the reserved word *class*, which should be followed by a valid identifier. After the identifier, everything else should be within curly braces. There can be various combinations inside these two curly braces. Two common building blocks of a class definition are fields and methods, as demonstrated in Figure 3.1. We will see various combinations throughout this book.

3.3 Object Definitions

Objects in Scala are singletons. If we have static methods and variables, we can make use of objects, instead of classes. Static methods and variables do not change based on an instance of a class. For example, the method to calculate a logarithm doesn't change; the process to calculate a logarithm is a fixed process.

Object definitions have the same structure as that of class definitions, except it starts with the reserved word *object*. Also if we need a runnable application, we need to have an object with a main method. Alternatively, we could extend *Application* class and avoid writing the main method. By now, we have seen many object definitions, starting from Chapter 1.

3.4 Conclusion

In this chapter, we discussed classes and objects. We covered two important class members—fields and methods. A field holds a state related value of an object and a method represents a behavior of an object. Further, we discussed class definition as well as object definition.

3.5 Review Questions

1. What is a major difference between a class and an object?
2. Is it possible to write a Scala program without a class?
3. Is a class a runnable application by itself?
4. How can we run a class?
5. What are singleton objects?
6. When a class is instantiated multiple times and assigned to different identifiers, do those instances have the same memory location?
7. When should a class be created?
8. Why it is important to create a class?
9. What is a case class?

3.6 Problems

1. Create a class called *Rectangle* with three fields: *length*, *breadth*, and *area*. Also write a method called *computeArea* in the *Rectangle* class. Next, create a rectangle application called *RectApplication*, which provides length and breadth, invokes *computeArea* method and prints the area, on the console.
2. Solve Problem #1 with a case class and a singleton object.
3. Create a class called *Book* that has three fields: *name*, *price*, and *quantity*. The field *price* is of type *Price* that has two fields in it: *currencyName* and *priceValue*. Next, create a runnable application to print the total price of given quantities of a book. Create the remaining classes and methods, appropriately.

3.7 Answers to Review Questions

1. A major difference between a class and an object is that a class is a template or a blueprint and an object is an instance of a class.
2. Yes, it is possible to write a Scala program without a class.
3. No, class cannot be run directly.

4. In order to run a class, a singleton object with a main method should be created. Next, the class should be instantiated inside this singleton object. Once instantiated, public fields and methods are accessible from the singleton object.

5. As the name suggests, singleton objects have only one instance. They are used to house methods and fields of static nature, i.e., they do not change based on class instances. When a singleton object shares the same name as that of a class, it is called a companion object; a companion object should be defined in the same source file.

6. No, different instances assigned to different identifiers have different memory locations.

7. A class should be created when there is a need for a blueprint. A good test is that you need multiple instances of this class.

8. It is important to create a class, because it has several advantages: it is a modular code so that maintenance becomes cost effective; it can be re-used as many times as needed and hence reduces the cost of development as well as maintenance; it is a natural representation of real world classes and classifications.

9. A case class is a model, i.e., it has only fields; getters and setters are auto-generated during compilation.

3.8 Solutions to Problems

1. ```
class Rectangle {
    var length = 0
    var breadth = 0
    var area = 0
    def computeArea(): Unit = {
        area = length * breadth
    }
}

object RectApplication {
    def main(args: Array[String]): Unit = {
        val rectObj = new Rectangle
        rectObj.length = 4
        rectObj.breadth = 5
        rectObj.computeArea()
        println(rectObj.area)
    }
}
```
```

2. `case class RectangleCase(length: Int, breadth: Int)`

```scala
object RectangleWithCase {
   def main(args: Array[String]): Unit = {
      val rectObj = new RectangleCase (4, 5)
      val area = rectObj.length * rectObj.breadth
      println (area)
   }
}
```

3. `case class Price(currencyName: String, priceValue: Double)`

```scala
class Book {
   var name: String = ""
   var price: Price = null
   var quantity = 0
   var totalPrice = 0.0
   def computeTotalPrice(): Unit = {
      totalPrice = price.priceValue * quantity
   }
}

object BookApp {
   def main(args: Array[String]): Unit = {
      val priceOfBook = Price("USD", 25.5)
      val bookObj = new Book
      bookObj.name = "Programming with Scala"
      bookObj.price = priceOfBook
      bookObj.quantity = 4
      bookObj.computeTotalPrice()
      println(bookObj.price.currencyName+" "+bookObj.totalPrice)
   }
}
```

Chapter 4
Control Structures

In our daily lives, we have a flow of activities. In a particular day, we do a series of things and it is fair to say that we make several choices consciously or unconsciously. Also it may not be inaccurate to say that we repeat things on a daily basis. So there are several questions to ask ourselves—*How do we make decisions regarding choices? How do we decide whether to repeat something? How do we decide the flow of activities on a particular day? What guides the flow of activities during a day? What guides the flow of activities in an individual's life? Can we change our daily activities without affecting our long term goals?* All of these questions can be related to programming. Our mind can be thought of as a combination of memory and a processing unit and rest of the body as an implementation agent. And of course, we get help from other people and machines to achieve our goals. The nature of computer programming is not much different from this scenario.

The Scala programming language allows us to express controlling elements with the help of control structures. The *conditional expression*, as the name suggests, is to express flow that has conditional choices. For example, if the price of the house is less than $5M, buy the house, otherwise look for other houses that match the price criteria. A *for expression* is a powerful way of expressing repeats; they have fine controls available, which we will see later in this chapter. Similarly, a *while loop* is a natural way to express while conditions. Exceptions occur when a program encounters unexpected values. This situation can be handled using a feature called *exception handling*.

4.1 Conditional Expressions

Conditional expressions, also known as if-else expressions, direct the program execution flow based on the result of evaluation of a test condition. If the result is true, one branch of code is executed, otherwise the other branch of code is executed. Figure 4.1 shows how to use a conditional expression. The program reads a number from a keyboard and prints whether the input number is less than 5, or greater than

© Springer International Publishing AG 2017
B.P. Upadhyaya, *Programming with Scala*, Undergraduate
Topics in Computer Science, https://doi.org/10.1007/978-3-319-69368-2_4

or equal to 5. *If* is followed by a condition in parentheses, then a block of code to be executed, if the condition evaluates to true. After that we have *else*, which is followed by a block of code to be executed, if the condition evaluates to false. Please note that the curly braces are optional if there is only one statement to be executed.

```scala
object IfElse {
    def main(args: Array[String]): Unit = {
        println("Enter a number: ")
        val inputNumber = scala.io.StdIn.readInt()
        if (inputNumber < 5)
            println("Number is smaller than 5")
        else
            println("Number is greater than or equal to 5")
    }
}
```

Fig. 4.1: If Expression

Now, let's take a slightly different example. Figure 4.2 shows an *if-else-if-else* structure. We can have any number of *else-if* in the if-structure. Also please note the curly braces this time; these are required except for the last *else*, which has only one statement. This program prints the positive difference between two numbers, irrespective of the order of entry. If the numbers are equal the execution will fall into the block that checks only the flag value and hence it will print *Two numbers are equal*. It might look a bit non-intuitive initially, but the previous two tests check the inequality, and the only remaining case is the equality case.

The *if* structure in this case has multiple conditions. First it checks whether the flag is set to true, and then it checks whether the difference is greater than 0. The else does the same but the order of the numbers are different for the difference calculation.

```scala
import scala.io.StdIn._
object PositiveDifference {
    def main(args: Array[String]): Unit = {
        var positiveDiff = 0
        val executeFlag = true
        print("Please enter first number: ")
        val firstNumber = readInt()
        print("Please enter second number: ")
        val secondNumber = readInt()
        if((executeFlag == true) &&
          (firstNumber - secondNumber) > 0) {
            positiveDiff = firstNumber - secondNumber
            println("The positive difference: "+positiveDiff)
        } else if((executeFlag == true) &&
          (secondNumber - firstNumber) > 0) {
            positiveDiff = secondNumber - firstNumber
            println("The positive difference: "+ positiveDiff)
        } else if(executeFlag == true) {
            println("Two numbers are equal")
        } else {
            println("The execution flag is not set")
        }
    }
}
```

Fig. 4.2: If Expression - Positive Difference

4.2 For Expressions

A for expression or for control structure is one of the most widely used control structures. Also many professional programmers have the same opinion about it: it is a powerful control structure. Let's start with a simple for loop. Figure 4.3 shows a program to detect a prime number. The for expression, in this program, has two parts for variable control. i is the variable and it starts with value 2 and ends at value $number - 1$. All the statements to be executed are enclosed in curly braces.

The logic to calculate whether a number is prime or not comes from our knowledge of mathematics. If a number is divisible only by 1 and by itself, then it is a prime number. The operator % gives the remainder; so, $5\%3 = 2$.

Now, let's look at the *for expression* variations. *for(i <- 1 until 5) print(i)* prints 1, 2, 3, and 4. With until, if we have n as the upper limit, it goes up to $n - 1$. Next, you are advised to look at the short programs below and experiment with the variations on your own.

```scala
object PrimeNumberDetection {
    def main(args: Array[String]): Unit = {
        print("Please enter an integer: ")
        val number = scala.io.StdIn.readInt()
        var prime = true
        for(i <- 2 to number - 1) {
            if (number % i == 0) {
                prime = false
            }
        }
        if(prime) {
            println("The number "+number+" is prime.")
        } else {
            println("The number "+number+" is not prime.")
        }
    }
}
```

Fig. 4.3: Prime Number Detection

1.
```scala
object ForExperiment1 {
    def main(args: Array[String]): Unit = {
        for(i <- 1 until 5)
            print(i+", ")
    }
}
// Output: 1, 2, 3, 4,
```

2.
```scala
object ForExperiment2 {
    def main(args: Array[String]): Unit = {
        for(i <- (1 to 5).reverse)
            print(i+", ")
    }
}
// Output: 5, 4, 3, 2, 1,
```

3.
```scala
object ForExperiment3 {
    def main(args: Array[String]): Unit = {
        for(i <- 5 to 1 by -1)
            print(i+", ")
    }
}
// Output: 5, 4, 3, 2, 1,
```

4.
```scala
object ForExperiment4 {
    def main(args: Array[String]): Unit = {
        for(i <- 1 to 3; j <- 1 to 2)
            print(i+","+j+"; ")
    }
}
// Output: 1,1; 1,2; 2,1; 2,2; 3,1; 3,2;
```

5.
```scala
object ForExperiment5 {
    def main(args: Array[String]): Unit = {
    for(i <- 1 to 4; if i != 3; j <- 1 to 4; if i != j)
        print(i+","+j+"; ")
    }
}
// Output: 1,2; 1,3; 1,4; 2,1; 2,3; 2,4; 4,1; 4,2; 4,3;
```

6.
```scala
object ForExperiment6 {
    def main(args: Array[String]): Unit = {
    for(i <- 1 to 4; startJ = 5 - i; j <- startJ to 4)
        print(i+","+j+"; ")
    }
}
// Output: 1,4; 2,3; 2,4; 3,2; 3,3; 3,4; 4,1; 4,2; 4,3; 4,4;
```

7.
```scala
object ForExperiment7 {
    def main(args: Array[String]): Unit = {
        val square = for(i <- 1 to 4) yield i * i
        print(square)
    }
}
// Output: Vector(1, 4, 9, 16)
```

8.
```scala
object ForExperiment8 {
    def main(args: Array[String]): Unit = {
        print(sum(3,4,5))
    }

    def sum(args: Int*): Int = {
        var sum = 0
        for (num <- args) {
            sum += num
        }
        sum
    }
}
// Output: 12
```

9.
```scala
object ForExperiment9 {
    def main(args: Array[String]): Unit = {
        print(sumOfEvenNumbers(1,2,3,4,5))
    }

    def sumOfEvenNumbers(numbers: Int*): Int = {
        var sum = 0
        for(num <- numbers if num % 2 == 0) {
            sum += num
        }
        sum
    }
}
//Output: 6
```

4.3 While Loops

The general structure of the while loop is *while (<condition >){<statements >}*.
First, the condition is evaluated; if it is true, then the code within curly braces is
executed. After the first iteration, the condition is re-evaluated; if it is true, then the
code within curly braces is executed again. This keeps repeating until the condition
is false. When it is false the code within curly braces is skipped and the program
execution moves to the LOC immediately after the closing curly brace.

```
object PrimeNumbersUsingWhile {
    def main(args: Array[String]): Unit = {
        print("Please enter a number: ")
        val inputNumber = scala.io.StdIn.readInt()
        var isPrime = true
        var i = 2
        while(i < inputNumber) {
            if(inputNumber % i == 0) {
                isPrime = false
            }
            i += 1
        }
        if(isPrime) {
            println("The number "+inputNumber+" is prime")
        } else {
            println("The number "+inputNumber+" is not prime")
        }
    }
}
```

Fig. 4.4: Prime Number Detection using While

Figure 4.4 presents a prime number detection program using a while loop. Compare Figure 4.4 and Figure 4.3. A *for expression* has initialization as a part of the
expression, whereas a *while loop* has a separate LOC for initialization. Usually it
should come before the *while loop*. Also in case of *while*, the loop variable increment is done with a separate LOC, whereas *for* has implicit increments, i. e., it
increases automatically by 1.

While loops are natural when the final condition check is to be highlighted. One
loop can be converted to another with some effort. But you might have noticed that
a for expression has many options available. Also it is considered one of the most
powerful control structures by industrial programmers, specifically in an imperative
programming domain. Please note that *for* is called an expression but *while* is called
a loop. This is because *while* does not return an interesting value. The type of result
we get from *while* is Unit.

Scala has a *do-while* structure as well. The major difference between *while* and
do-while is that the statements in *do-while* are executed at least once, regardless
of the result of evaluation of the condition. So, if we know beforehand that the

statements should be executed at least once, then *do-while* is the choice. The code
fragment below prints *1,2,3,4,*. If we alter the condition to *i* >*5*, it still prints *1,,*
because the condition is tested after the first iteration.

```
var i = 1
do {
    print(i+",")
    i += 1
} while( i < 5)
```

4.4 Exception Handling

Exception handling is a mechanism that saves programs from crashing during run
time. Since programmers may not know all the possible values that users of a program supply during run time, there might be a situation when the program does not
know how to handle the values. If this occurs, it might make the program crash. A
program or an application crashing during run time is undesirable. It makes customers run away from that application. So a software engineer has to do everything
possible to not let a program or an application crash during run time. If a program
cannot handle certain situations or values, it has to gracefully terminate.

```
object ExceptionDemo1 {
    def main(args: Array[String]): Unit = {
        print("Please enter a number: ")
        try {
            val inputNumber = scala.io.StdIn.readInt()
            println("It was a valid input: "+inputNumber)
        } catch {
            case ex: NumberFormatException =>
             println("Type mismatch")
            case ex: Exception => println("Something went wrong")
        } finally {
            println("Exiting gracefully from main method")
        }
    }
}
```

Fig. 4.5: Exception Handling

Figure 4.5 demonstrates the structure of exception handling. It has a *try* {...}
catch {...} *finally* {...} structure. It is intuitive; we try certain operations and we ex-
pect some exceptional condition, which is then caught within the *catch* block and
handled. *finally* is used to execute statements, which should be executed irrespective of whether an exception occurred or not. For example, if we open an I/O file
successfully but something goes wrong during parsing and we cannot continue, then

there will be an exception. We might let the user know that with an appropriate message in the *catch* block. Now, whether the file is successfully processed or not, we still have to close the file to prevent dangling references or memory leakage. This is taken care of by closing the file in the *finally* block.

The program shown in Figure 4.5 throws an exception if the user enters data that is not an integer. For example, if the user enters a string instead of an integer value, it throws *NumberFormatException*. That's exactly what we are catching in the *catch* block. Also there might be other sources of exception, so to cover that we have a more generic case listed, *Exception*. The message for the first case is very specific, which is more helpful. For the second message, we might need to see the stack trace and figure out what specific thing went wrong. Further, in the *catch* block, we see lambda expressions, which we will discuss in detail later, when we study functions. For now, it is sufficient to understand that if a type mismatch occurs, we get *NumberFormatException*, which matches with the first case, in the *catch* block, and that results in the execution of the statement on the right side of =>.

Now, let's take one more example of exception handling, as it is an important feature for professional work. Figure 4.6 demonstrates how to throw an exception. Also it demonstrates how to catch that exception in the calling method. The method *performDivision* checks whether the denominator is 0 or not. If it is 0, it throws *RuntimeException*, which is then propagated to the calling method, which is *main*, in this case. When division by 0 occurs, it matches with the second case in the *catch* block, which gets original message using the handler *ex*. The rest of the program elements were discussed earlier.

```scala
import scala.io.StdIn._
object ExceptionDemo2 {
   def main(args: Array[String]): Unit = {
      try {
         print("Enter the first integer: ")
         val firstNumber = readInt()
         print("Enter the second integer: ")
         val secondNumber = readInt()
         val quotient =
          performDivision(firstNumber,secondNumber)
         println("Quotient: "+quotient)
      } catch {
         case ex: NumberFormatException =>
          println("Type mismatch")
         case ex: RuntimeException => println(ex.getMessage)
         case ex: Exception => println("Something went wrong")
      }
   }

   def performDivision(num1: Int, num2: Int): Int = {
      var result = 0
      if(num2 == 0) {
         throw new RuntimeException("Division by zero")
      } else {
         result = num1 / num2
      }
      result
   }
}
```

Fig. 4.6: Exception Handling with Custom Throw

4.5 Conclusion

In this chapter, we discussed if-expressions, which are frequently used. Then we explored one of the most widely used control structures, for-expression. It is considered to be one of the most powerful control structures by professional programmers. Also we presented numerous variations of the for-expression. We covered while-loops, including the do-while structure. Finally, we discussed a feature to prevent an application from crashing, i. e., exception handling. We also covered exception propagation.

4.6 Review Questions

1. Is it syntactically correct to have an if-else structure inside another if-else structure?

2. In for-expressions, what is the difference between *until* and *to*?
3. In for-expressions, is it possible to have multiple loop control variables?
4. If a while-loop condition is false, are statements within the loop executed at least once?
5. What is one major difference between *while* loops and *do-while* loops?
6. What is the importance of exception handling?
7. Is it possible to propagate an exception from one method to another method?
8. Is it possible to propagate an exception from one object to another object?

4.7 Problems

1. Using for-expressions, write a program to generate Fibonacci numbers less than 40. Include 0 as well. Hint: Fibonacci numbers can be generated using the formula: $F_n = F_{n-1} + F_{n-2}$.
2. Use a while-loop to solve Problem #1.
3. Read an integer between 1 and 10, inclusive, from the keyboard. Then generate Fibonacci numbers greater than this integer. The generated numbers should be less than 30 and the program should print appropriate messages for exceptions. Throw an appropriate exception for out of range inputs.
4. Write a program to calculate the factorial of a given non-negative number.

4.8 Answers to Review Questions

1. Yes, it is syntactically correct to have an if-else structure inside another if-else structure. Theoretically, there is not limit on this.
2. In for-expressions, if we use *until*, it goes up to $n - 1$; if we use *to*, it goes up to n. For the same starting value and the same increment, *until* loops one less time compared with *to*.
3. Yes, it is possible to have multiple loop control variables in for-expressions.
4. In a while-loop, statements are not executed if the condition is false.
5. One major difference between *while* loops and *do-while* loops is that statements are executed at least once in *do-while* but this is not true for *while* loops.
6. Exception handling is a mechanism that prevents an application from crashing.
7. Yes, it is possible to propagate an exception from one method to another. By having a *throw* clause in the called method, an exception can be propagated to the caller method. It is important to catch this propagated exception in the caller, otherwise the application crashes.
8. Yes, since methods are associated with objects, propagating exceptions at the method level is equivalent to propagating exceptions at the object level.

4.9 Solutions to Problems

1.
```scala
object FibonacciWithFor {
    def main(args: Array[String]): Unit = {
        generateFibonacciSeries
    }

    def generateFibonacciSeries: Unit = {
        var f0 = 0
        var f1 = 1
        var fn = 0
        print(f0+", ")
        for (i <- 0 until 40) {
            fn = f0 + f1
            if (fn >= 40)
                return
            print(fn + ", ")
            f0 = f1
            f1 = fn
        }
    }
}
```

2.
```scala
object FibonacciWithWhile {
    def main(args: Array[String]): Unit = {
        generateFibonacciSeries
    }

    def generateFibonacciSeries: Unit = {
        var f0 = 0
        var f1 = 1
        var fn = 0
        print(fn+", ")
        while(fn < 34) {
            fn = f0 + f1
            print(fn+", ")
            f0 = f1
            f1 = fn
        }
    }
}
```

3.
```scala
object FibonacciCustom {
    def main(args: Array[String]): Unit = {
        print("Please enter an integer between 1 and 10: ")
        try {
            val inputNumber = scala.io.StdIn.readInt()
            if (inputNumber < 0  || inputNumber > 10) {
                throw new RuntimeException("Number out of range!")
            }
            generateCustomFibonacci(inputNumber)
        } catch {
            case e : NumberFormatException =>
             println("Type mismatch!")
            case e: RuntimeException => println(e.getMessage)
            case e: Exception => println("Something went wrong")
        }
    }

    def generateCustomFibonacci(num: Int): Unit = {
        var f0 = 0
        var f1 = 1
        var fn = f0 + f1
        for(i <- 0 to 10) {
            if(fn > num && fn < 30) {
                print(fn+", ")
            }
            f0 = f1
            f1 = fn
            fn = f0 + f1
        }
    }
}
```

4.
```scala
object Factorial {
    def main(args: Array[String]): Unit = {
        print("Please enter a non-negative integer: ")
        try {
            val inputNumber = scala.io.StdIn.readInt()
            val factorial = calculateFactorial(inputNumber)
            println("The factorial of "+inputNumber+" is "+
              factorial+".")
        } catch {
            case e: NumberFormatException =>
             println("Type mismatch!")
            case e: RuntimeException => println(e.getMessage)
            case e: Exception => println("Something went wrong!")
        }
    }

    def calculateFactorial(num: Int): Long = {
        var product = 1
        if(num < 0) {
            throw new RuntimeException("Number is negative!")
        }
        var i = num
        while(i >= 1) {
            product *= i
            i -= 1
        }
        product
    }
}
```

Chapter 5
Operators

Operators provide us with mechanisms to process values. A typical computer is mostly about processing values. In isolation, operators look simple, but when combined with other building blocks of Scala, they can quickly result in a complex program. So it is important to pay good attention. Scala has wide variety of operators and these operators are method calls. This is different from many other programming languages that we discussed briefly in Chapter 1.

5.1 Operators as Methods

Scala operators work as methods, as shown in Figure 5.1. The first two variables a and b are assigned integer values 2 and 3, respectively. Scala type inference assigns type *Int* to both a and b. *scala.Int* class has over a hundred methods and $+$ is one of those. So, $+$ can be used both as an infix operator or as a method. Identifier c is assigned value 5, after evaluating the right-hand side expression. With similar reasoning, d and e have exactly the same value, 6. The last one shows *indexOf* method being used as an operator. So f gets value 4, because string indexing starts with 0.

Let's look at some unary operators now. The expression *2.unary_-* is equivalent to -2. The identifiers that can be used as prefix operators are:

    $+$ $-$ $!$ $\sim$

The exclamation sign is a logical inversion and tilde is a binary bit inversion. So, *(! true)* is evaluated to *false*.

Figure 5.2 demonstrates how to write a custom operator. This is one of the strengths of Scala. We can develop our own domain specific language. For this particular example, we would like to have an operator that takes two strings, swaps them, and then joins them. For that, we define a class called *MyData* that has this operator method, *<->+*, which performs swap and join. In the application, object *CustomMethodAsOperator*, we create an instance of *MyData*. In the next LOC, we

© Springer International Publishing AG 2017

B.P. Upadhyaya, *Programming with Scala*, Undergraduate
Topics in Computer Science, https://doi.org/10.1007/978-3-319-69368-2_5

```
object OperatorsDemo {
def main(args: Array[String]): Unit = {
   val a = 2
   val b = 3
   val c = a.+(b)
   println(c)
   val d = 3 + 3L
   val e = 3.+(3L)
   println(d,e)
   val name = "Mountain"
   val f = name indexOf 't'
   println(f)
   }
}
```

Fig. 5.1: Operators as Methods

apply the operator with parameter "05". Finally, we print the result; it prints *05-2017*. By now, you might have realized the strength of this. Think of creating your own SQL, or a programming language that you think better reflects your organization's needs. For this reason, Scala is also called a meta-language, i.e., a language about language.

```
object CustomMethodAsOperator {
   def main(args: Array[String]): Unit = {
      val year = new MyData("2017")
      println(year <->+ "05")
   }
}

class MyData (item1: String) {
   def <->+(item2: String): String = {
      val newString = item2.concat("-").concat(item1)
      newString
   }
}
```

Fig. 5.2: Custom Operators as Methods

5.2 Arithmetic Operators

Addition, subtraction, multiplication, and division are arithmetic operations. The operators to perform these operations are +, -, *, and /, respectively. Also the remainder operator, %, is available to calculate a remainder. We make use of the Scala interpreter to see how these operators work, as writing a complete program consumes more space, and repeats many elements that you have already seen numerous times in this book. The following code snippet shows the Scala interpreter. *scala>* means we are in Scala interpreter mode and REPL (Read-Evaluate-Print Loop) is available.

```
scala> 3 + 2
res0: Int = 5
```

One of the advantages of Scala REPL is that we don't have to open an IDE and write a complete program to see the output. It is an efficient way to test Scala features. $3 + 2$ is an expression and Scala interpreter knows how to evaluate this. We don't have to necessarily assign a variable, which is different if we are using IDEs like Scala IDE, intelliJ, Eclipse, etc. IDEs require us to provide an identifier as well. Here, $3 + 2$ is evaluated and assigned to an identifier by the Scala interpreter. *res0: Int =5* is the output of our expression. The interpreter created an identifier *res0* and assigned the result of expression $3 + 2$.

```
scala> 3 - 2
res1: Int = 1
```

Now, it should be fairly intuitive. This time the interpreter created identifier *res1* for us. Also it evaluated the expression $3 - 2$ and assigned the result to the newly created variable. Please note that the type was automatically inferred based upon our expression.

If we type *res0* in the interpreter, the value is still available. When it prints, it assigns it to a new identifier as shown below.

```
scala> res0
res2: Int = 5
```

Now, let's look at some more arithmetic operations. $3/2$ gives us the quotient of 3 divided by 2, whereas 5%3 gives us the remainder of 5 divided by 3. Similarly, we can simply write -5 as the subtraction operator can be used as a unary operator. If we supply our own identifier, Scala uses that instead of creating its own.

```
scala> 3 / 2
res4: Int = 1

scala> 5 % 3
res5: Int = 2

scala> -5
res7: Int = -5

scala> val a = 5
a: Int = 5
```

5.3 Relational and Logical Operators

Relational operators help us to compare values. Scala has greater than ($>$), less than ($<$), greater than or equal to ($>=$), and less than or equal to ($<=$) operators for relational processing. When evaluated, these operators result in a boolean value. Let's look at some examples.

```
scala> 1 > 4.5
res8: Boolean = false

scala> 'z' == 'Z'
res11: Boolean = false

scala> ("Prog"+"ramming") == "Programming"
res13: Boolean = true

scala> ! true
res18: Boolean = false
```

The first example compared an integer with a floating point number. Interpreter is capable enough to do conversion and comparison. Since 1 is not greater than 4.5, it evaluates to false. Similarly, 'z' and 'Z' have different unicode and they are not the same, and hence the result is false. The third case is an example of object equality. Scala allows to compare two objects with the == operator. The values of the objects are compared and hence we have the result as true. Finally, we have an example of unary operator, (! true) is false.

Scala has logical operators or logical methods to perform logical operations: logical-and (&&) and logical-or(||). Logical operators differentiate themselves from relational operators by taking *Boolean* operands; the result is *Boolean* too. Now, let's look at some examples.

```
scala> true && true
res20: Boolean true

scala> true && false
res21: Boolean = false

scala> false || true
res22: Boolean = true
```

Table 5.1 presents a truth table for logical-and and logical-or. So (true && true) should evaluate to true, which is exactly what we see in the Scala interpreter. The remaining two examples also match the truth table values. Details of *Boolean* logic are available in *An Investigation of the Laws of Thought* by George Boole [Boo05].

Table 5.1: Truth Table for Logical Operators

Operand 1	Operand 2	Logical AND	Logical OR
true	true	true	true
true	false	false	true
false	true	false	true
false	false	false	false

5.4 Bitwise Operators

Bitwise manipulation may not look like a commonly used feature for typical application programming work. But it allows low level manipulation of data, which makes it a powerful feature. Cryptography is one area that uses bit manipulation. Also, if we are implementing security libraries this feature might prove handy. In any case, it is a good engineering exercise to work with bits. Sometimes, new application areas emerge and certain features of a programming language are in high demand.

Table 5.2 shows the truth table for bitwise operators. If we represent operand 1 with x and operand 2 with y, *AND or* & is equivalent to the product of x and y. Similarly, *OR or* | is equivalent to special addition, denoted by $\overline{+}$. For special addition: $0\overline{+}0 = 0$, $0\overline{+}1 = 1$, $1\overline{+}0 = 1$, and $1\overline{+}1 = 1$. *XOR or* ^ can be calculated with the equation $x\overline{y} + \overline{x}y$.

Table 5.2: Truth Table for Bitwise Operators

Operand 1 (x)	Operand 2 (y)	AND $(x.y)$	OR $(x\overline{+}y)$	XOR $(x \oplus y)$
true	true	true	true	false
true	false	false	true	true
false	true	false	true	true
false	false	false	false	false

In order to complement a bit, Scala provides a unary operator, tilde (~). Sometimes, we need to shift bits left or right. For that, Scala provides shift left ($<<$), shift right ($>>$), and unsigned shift right($>>>$). Now, let's look at some examples.

```
scala> 1 & 2
res27: Int = 0

scala> 1 | 2
res28: Int = 3
```

```
scala> 1 ^ 2
res29: Int = 3

scala> ~1
res37: Int = -2

scala> 1 << 2
res30: Int = 4

scala> 1 >> 2
res31: Int = 0

scala> 1 >>> 2
res32: Int = 0
```

In the first example, $1 \& 2 = 0$, because for a 32-bit representation 1 is (0000 0000 0000 0000 0000 0000 0000 0001) and 2 is (0000 0000 0000 0000 0000 0000 0000 0010). When we do bitwise *AND* we get (0000 0000 0000 0000 0000 0000 0000 0000), which is 0. Applying the same logic, $1|2$ evaluates to integer value 3. Now, for the unary operator tilde, using 32-bit representation, (~1) becomes (1111 1111 1111 1111 1111 1111 1111 1110), which is -2.

How about shift operators? Let's analyze $1 << 2 = 4$. We know that the 32-bit representation for 1 is (0000 0000 0000 0000 0000 0000 0000 0001). The number after the shift operator tells us how many times to shift. Since it is shift left, we shift bits to the left by 2 positions. Now, it becomes (0000 0000 0000 0000 0000 0000 0000 0100), which is integer value 4.

We apply the same logic to the last two examples. When we shift (0000 0000 0000 0000 0000 0000 0000 0001) by 2 positions right, it becomes (0000 0000 0000 0000 0000 0000 0000 0000) and hence 0. The last example shows shift right operation for unsigned numbers, that means there is no sign bit consideration. Since 1 is a positive number, its sign bit is 0. When we shift right by 2 positions, we get all 0s, which is 0 again.

High-tech companies like Apple, Google, Amazon, Intel, etc., do low-level programming. The ultimate power comes with low level programming. Even if you are doing projects in an academic setting, low level features will be useful, especially when you are involved in deep engineering.

5.5 Operator Precedence and Associativity

Operator precedence is one of the important fundamentals of the Scala programming language. It determines the order of evaluation of different parts of an expression. Unintended order can easily produce incorrect results. Table 5.3 shows a list of operators from highest to lowest precedence.

Table 5.3: Operator Precedence

SN	Operators
1	An operator character other than listed below. (Highest precedence)
2	* / %
3	+ -
4	:
5	= !
6	< >
7	&
8	^
9	|
10	All letters
11	Assignment operators. (Lowest precedence)

Let's take an example. If we execute $5 + 5 * 5$, in Scala interpreter, we get 30, not 50. Why is it so? It is because of precedence. Since multiplication has higher precedence than addition, the expression becomes $5 + (5 * 5)$. Also please note that parentheses have highest precedence.

```
scala> 5 + 5 * 5
res40: Int  30

scala> (5 + 5) * 5
res41: Int = 50
```

The associativity of operators determines how different parts of an expression are grouped together for calculation. Here are some rules to remember:

1. The last character in the operator/method determines the associativity.
2. If a method ends with ':', grouping is done from right to left.
3. If a method does not end with ':', grouping is done from left to right.

Based on the above rules, the expression $a * b * c$ is grouped as $(a * b) * c$. Please note that this is how Scala determines which part to evaluate first, if there are operators with the same precedence level. Now applying another rule, $x ::: y ::: z$ is grouped as $x ::: (y ::: z)$. Also $x ::: y$ becomes $y. ::: (x)$, right to left associativity. Let's remind ourselves, $2 + 3$ becomes $2. + (3)$, not $3. + (2)$; it is left to right associativity.

5.6 Conclusion

In this chapter, we started with operators as methods. Scala operators are method calls; this is the major point to remember. Then we covered arithmetic operators (or methods). We developed our own operator and applied that to process operands.

Relational and logical operators play important roles in programming, which was covered along with a truth table. Similarly, we covered bitwise operators, which are handy features if we are doing low level manipulation. Certain domains use low level programming more than other domains. Operator precedence and associativity determine the order in which different parts of an expression are evaluated.

5.7 Review Questions

1. Are Scala operators method calls?
2. What is the output of the expression $10\%3 == 1$?
3. Does 'a' == 'A' evaluate to true?
4. What is the output of the expression $(true \&\& false) \&\& (1<5||12>10)$?
5. What is the output of the expression $5 \char`^5$?
6. What is the output of the expression $((1>>2)+1) == ((1>>>2)+(\char`~1)+3)$?
7. Is $a ::: b$ equivalent to $a. ::: (b)$?
8. Convert $x * y * z$ to method call notation.

5.8 Problems

1. Using custom defined verb operators, create valid English sentences having the form *Subject+Verb+Object*. You can limit your scope to 2 subjects, 2 verbs, and 2 objects.
2. Modify the solution for Problem #1 so that sentences do not have any string in double quotes.
3. Let's assume that lower temperature implies higher probability of rain. Input city name and temperature for that city, from a keyboard, for two data points, and determine which city has higher probability of rain. Temperature range should be between 50°F and 80°F.

5.9 Answers to Review Questions

1. Yes, Scala operators are method calls. This is different from other programming languages that we discussed in Chapter 1.
2. true
3. No
4. false
5. 0
6. true
7. No. $a ::: b$ is equivalent to $b. ::: (a)$; it is right to left associative.

8. The method call notation for $x * y * z$ is $(x. * (y)). * (z)$; it is left to right associative.

5.10 Solutions to Problems

1.
```scala
object SimpleEnglishSentence {
    def main(args: Array[String]): Unit = {
        val I = new Subject("I")
        val You = new Subject("You")
        val sentence1 = I eat "rice"
        val sentence2 = You read "magazine"
    }
}

class Subject(subject: String) {
    def eat(anObject: String): String = {
        val sentence = subject.concat(" ").concat("eat")
         .concat(" ").concat(anObject).concat(".")
        sentence
    }

    def read(anObject: String): String = {
        val sentence = subject.concat(" ").concat("read")
         .concat(" ").concat(anObject).concat(".")
        sentence
    }
}
```

2.
```scala
case class Object(anObject: String)

object SimpleEnglishSentenceRefined {
   def main(args: Array[String]): Unit = {
      val I = new Subject1("I")
      val You = new Subject1("You")
      val rice = Object("rice")
      val magazine = Object("magazine")
      val sentence1 = I eat rice
      val sentence2 = You read magazine
   }
}

class Subject1(subject: String) {
   def eat(obj: Object): String = {
      val sentence = subject.concat(" ").concat("eat")
       .concat(" ").concat(obj.anObject).concat(".")
      sentence
   }

def read(obj: Object): String = {
   val sentence = subject.concat(" ").concat("read")
    .concat(" ").concat(obj.anObject).concat(".")
   sentence
}
}
```

3.
```scala
import scala.io.StdIn._
object WeatherForecast {
    def main(args: Array[String]): Unit = {
        forecastRain
    }

    def forecastRain: Unit = {
        try {
            print("Enter first city name: ")
            val city1Name = readLine()
            print("Enter temperature: ")
            val city1Temp = readFloat()
            if (city1Temp < 50 || city1Temp > 80) {
                throw new scala.RuntimeException(city1Name +
                  " temperature out of range.")
            }

            print("Enter second city name: ")
            val city2Name = readLine()
            print("Enter temperature: ")
            val city2Temp = readFloat()
            if (city2Temp < 50 || city2Temp > 80) {
                throw new scala.RuntimeException(city2Name +
                  " temperature out of range.")
            }

            if (city1Temp < city2Temp) {
            println(city1Name +
              " has higher probability of rain.")
            } else {
                println(city2Name +
                  "  has higher probability of rain.")
            }
        } catch {
            case e: NumberFormatException =>
             println("Type mismatch!")
            case e: RuntimeException => println(e.getMessage)
            case e: Exception => println("Something went wrong!")
        }
    }
}
```

Chapter 6
Data Input and Output

Generally users interact with computers using input and output devices. That means communication is data, i.e., either they supply data to computers or they consume data from computers. From the users' perspective data can be numbers, texts, images, graphs and other visualizations, etc. From the computers' perspective, all of this information is represented in terms of binary bits. Since it is monotonous to work with binary bits, high level programming languages like Scala provide a higher level representation, which is readable to the users. Character representation is a common understandable form. Also it provides finer control on textual as well as numeric representation.

In this chapter, we first discuss regular expressions, which provide us ways to process character level information. Then we discuss character level input and output. Also we cover character combinations like lines or strings. Once we process characters and lines, we need a way to group them together, which is a file system. So, we discuss reading from and writing to a file. Files can be located in many places, within an operating system. To cover this, finally, we discuss directory navigation.

6.1 Regular Expressions

Regular expressions originated from the work of S. C. Kleene [Kle56]. Scala makes it convenient to analyze data using the regular expression library, *scala.util.matching.Regex* class. Table 6.1 presents some of the notations supported by Scala, for a quick reference.

Let's take some examples to demonstrate how notations work in Scala. In order to use the regular expression library, we need to first import the Regex class as shown in the interpreter below. Then we define *anInteger* as a value that can optionally start with a − sign, which is followed by one or more digits. Next, we define our data called *data*, which is a string containing words, integers, and floating point numbers.

© Springer International Publishing AG 2017
B.P. Upadhyaya, *Programming with Scala*, Undergraduate
Topics in Computer Science, https://doi.org/10.1007/978-3-319-69368-2_6

Table 6.1: Regular Expression Notations

Notation	Meaning
+	One or more
?	Zero or one
*	Zero or more
-	Used for range
[]	Used for range
()	Used for character by character representation

The *findFirstIn* method locates the first occurrence, which is 44 in this case. Please note that type is *Option[String]* and the value is some value, *Some(44)*.

```scala
scala> import scala.util.matching.Regex
import scala.util.matching.Regex

scala> val anInteger = """(-)?(\d+)""".r
anInteger: scala.util.matching.Regex = (-)?(\d+)

scala> val data =
 "Scala programming 44 -55 is fun -1.1 3.4"
input: String =
 Scala programming 44 -55 is fun -1.1 3.4

scala> anInteger findFirstIn data
res1: Option[String] = Some(44)

scala> val aWord = """([a-zA-Z]+)""".r
aWord: scala.util.matching.Regex = ([a-zA-Z]+)

scala> aWord findFirstIn input
res17: Option[String] = Some(Scala)
```

Similarly, we define a regular expression for a word, *aWord*, which is one or more occurrence of letters 'a' to 'z' and 'A' to 'Z'. Next, we ask the interpreter to locate the first occurrence. The word "Scala" is the first word in our *data*, so it is a correct finding. By now, you must have realized that regular expressions provide rich string processing ability.

Next, let's write a complete program to demonstrate the use of regular expressions. In Figure 6.1, *data* has a string that contains words as well as numbers. We would like to extract money related numbers. For that, we define a regular expression called *moneyPattern*: starts with "USD", which is followed by one or more spaces, which is followed by one or more digits, which is optionally followed by

```
object RegularExpressions {
  def main(args: Array[String]): Unit = {
    val data =
      """
      | This is to demonstrate regular expressions.
      | My assets are 2 computers, 5 shirts, and
      | 35 books. Sometimes I eat USD 1.1 lunch, some
      | other times, it could be USD 2.5 lunch.
      """.stripMargin.toString

    val moneyPattern = """((USD)\s+)(\d+)(\.\d*)?""".r
    println((moneyPattern findAllIn data).toList)
  }
}
```

Fig. 6.1: Regular Expressions

a dot, and zero or more digits. There are two matches, and hence the output is *List(USD 1.1, USD 2.5)*.

6.2 Single Character Input

You might be wondering why we have a separate section for single character input. The primary reason is that it is a fall back method when other methods do not work. In practice, you might be reading a whole string or a line at a time, as far as application programming is concerned. For memory sensitive devices, character by character calculation is important; also the range of numerals is equally important.

Another reason for handling input character by character is transmission. If there is a limited bandwidth then it is practical to adjust the optimum number of characters. For example, there could be small field devices placed on farmland, which are capable of receiving small amounts of data. Further these devices may be capable of continuing transmission from the last successful transmission. In this kind of systems, byte level reading and writing becomes a practical solution.

```scala
object SingleCharInput {
    def main(args: Array[String]): Unit = {
        println("Enter each character followed by return key: ")
        val totalAvailableChars = 4
        var inputChar = ' '
        val inputBuffer = new Array[Char](totalAvailableChars)
        var i = 0
        while(i < totalAvailableChars) {
            inputChar = scala.io.StdIn.readChar()
            inputBuffer(i) = inputChar
            i += 1
        }
        inputBuffer.foreach(print)
    }
}
```

Fig. 6.2: Character Level Input and Output

Figure 6.2 shows how to limit the total space in terms of the number of available characters in the buffer. The *Array* size can be fixed by passing the total number of characters to be accommodated. While reading characters from a keyboard, you can control that with a loop variable. For your system, if a character is assigned 16 bits, you are allocating a total of 64 bits, which is equal to 8 bytes. If you are programming for a device that has limited memory, you need to calculate precisely.

Sometimes, we need to read a file byte by byte. In that case, you might like to allocate space accordingly, as shown in the code snippet below. Let's say you are programming for some embedded devices and file size should not be greater than 2 MB, then the space allocation would be something like:

```scala
val inputBuffer = new Array[Byte](2 * 1024)
```

6.3 Single Character Output

Analogous to single character input, single character output is used when character level control is required. Let's say we need to send a message to field devices located thousands of miles away from host servers and these devices have limited memory as well as limited bandwidth for transmission. In this case, engineers will be required to split data into smaller chunks which can be transmitted within available bandwidth. Also the overall size of data is limited.

```scala
object SingleCharOutput {
    def main(args: Array[String]): Unit = {
        val dataToTransmit =
            """
            | Soil moisture is low.
            | Please open water valve.
            """.stripMargin.toString
        val totalChar = dataToTransmit.length
        val transmissionLimitInChar = 16
        val totalNumberOfChunks =
                    (totalChar / transmissionLimitInChar) + 1
        val outputBuffer = Array.ofDim[Char](
                    totalNumberOfChunks,
                    transmissionLimitInChar)
        val intermediateData = dataToTransmit.toCharArray
        var dataIndex = 0
        for(i <- 0 until totalNumberOfChunks;
                    j <- 0 until transmissionLimitInChar) {
            outputBuffer(i)(j) = intermediateData(dataIndex)
            if(dataIndex < (intermediateData.size - 1)) {
                dataIndex += 1
            }
        }
        outputBuffer foreach {chunk => chunk foreach print;
         println}
    }
}
```

Fig. 6.3: Character Level Output

Figure 6.3 first defines data to be transmitted, *dataToTransmit*. Let's assume that transmission is expensive and slow, which is a realistic assumption for certain farming devices, based on our experience. Further, let's assume that a 16-character chunk is the optimum chunk for transmission. In case the transmission fails, we need to repeat the failed 16 characters, not the entire transmission, because the system is capable of resuming transmission from the failure point; this is also a realistic assumption.

Next, we calculate the total number of chunks by dividing the total number of characters by the transmission length limit. Then we create an output buffer, which is a two-dimensional character array. The first dimension represents the chunks and the second dimension represents the contents of each chunk. So, the characters from the given string are now re-arranged, so that they can be transmitted. The last statement prints the *outputBuffer* contents, so that we can verify the data by visual inspection.

One of the reasons for taking string reference data is that it is one of the most widely used data formats. If you navigate a professional project written in any high level language, you are most likely to see some forms of strings. But embedded devices, on the other hand, have limited memory and transmission capabilities. For this reason, character level processing is required. Please note that this is just one of those application areas; there are numerous other areas where character level processing is preferred. For example, if you are doing some cryptographic work, you might need to process character by character.

6.4 Reading From a File

Reading data from a flat file is a common practice in many applications. If we look at many big data intensive applications like Facebook, Google, etc. we can find flat file applications. In fact, many open source applications emerged from Google, Facebook, Amazon, etc. Even though Apple is a more closed company, people who worked there for a long time came out and started large open source projects, including the leading Apache Software Foundation. One pioneering company in big data, Cloudera, open sourced most of its projects. As of today, big data applications process very large flat files: gigabytes to petabytes.

Figure 6.4 presents a program that reads data from a text file, line by line. We are making use of the Java library, so we have the corresponding import statement. Please note that Scala allows us to write multiple items in a single import statement. Once we declare the file path, we create source by supplying the file path name to *fromFile* method of *Source* class. The *for* expression prints each line separately. Since there are multiple sources of exceptions, we provide cases accordingly. If the file path is not correct, we get *FileNotFoundException*. Sometimes there can be a problem with an I/O device, which is caught by *IOException* case. Everything else falls into the last case, which is a broader exception case.

```
import java.io.{IOException, FileNotFoundException}
import scala.io.Source
object ReadFromTextFile {
    def main(args: Array[String]): Unit = {
        val fileName = "/Users/.../temp/InputFile.txt"
        var source: scala.io.BufferedSource = null
        try {
            source = Source.fromFile(fileName)
            for(line <- source.getLines()) {
                println(line)
            }
        } catch {
            case e: FileNotFoundException =>
             println("File not found.")
            case e: IOException => println("IO problem.")
            case e: Exception => println("Something went wrong.")
        } finally {
            source.close()
        }
    }
}
```

Fig. 6.4: Reading from a Text File

6.5 Writing to a File

Like reading from a file, writing to a file is a common operation that programmers
have to perform. Text files are common in certain areas like big data. Figure 6.5
shows a program that creates a text file called *OutputFile.txt* and writes a sentence
Scala is a purely OO language.

```
import java.io.{File, PrintWriter}
object WriteToTextFile {
    def main(args: Array[String]): Unit = {
        val outFileName = "/Users/.../temp/OutputFile.txt"
        var printWriter: PrintWriter = null
        try {
            printWriter = new PrintWriter(new File(outFileName))
            printWriter.write("Scala is a purely OO language.")
        } catch {
            case e: Exception => println("Something went wrong.")
        } finally {
            printWriter.close()
        }
    }
}
```

Fig. 6.5: Writing to a Text File

The first line in the main method defines the file path, including the file name. The second LOC creates an instance of *java.io.PrintWriter*, which has a *write* method in it that can be called to write contents in the file. That is what is being done inside *try-catch* block. Then we are catching a generic exception, which covers all types of exceptions. Finally, we close the *printWriter*.

6.6 Navigating Directories

Directory operation is a handy feature when we need to organize our data in I/O devices. This is a common operation in many practical application domains. Figure 6.6 presents a program to list files in a directory and to list sub directories of a directory.

```
import java.io.File
object NavigatingDirectories {
    def main(args: Array[String]): Unit = {
        printListOfFilesInDirectory
        printListOfSubDirectories
    }

    def printListOfFilesInDirectory: Unit = {
        val dirName = "/Users/.../temp"
        val dir = new File(dirName)
        var listOfFiles: List[File] = null
        if (dir.exists() && dir.isDirectory) {
            listOfFiles = dir.listFiles.filter(_.isFile).toList
        } else {
            listOfFiles = List[File]()
        }
        listOfFiles.foreach(println)
    }

    def printListOfSubDirectories: Unit = {
        val dirName = "/Users/.../temp"
        val dir = new File(dirName)
        var listOfSubDirectories: List[String] = null
        listOfSubDirectories =
                dir.listFiles.filter(_.isDirectory).
            map(_.getName).toList
        listOfSubDirectories foreach println
    }
}
```

Fig. 6.6: Directory Navigation

This program utilizes *java.io.File* and hence we have a corresponding import. The main method invokes two other methods, which perform file listing and directory listing. In *printListOfFilesInDirectory* method, first we define a value for the directory path. The three dots in the middle of the directory path means you can insert the username for your machine if you are using Apple's Mac OS; it should be similar for Linux flavors. For Windows, you can start with a drive letter (like C:\).

A value *dir* is created by instantiating *File*, which takes the directory path as a parameter. Then we create a place holder variable called *listOfFiles* to hold the list of files. The if-condition checks two things: whether the directory exists and if it is a directory. If both the conditions are satisfied then appropriate methods are invoked on the object *dir*. Please note the *listFiles* method lists both files and directories; so we need to filter them appropriately. The underscore represents any item returned by method *listFiles*. Finally, the filtered items are converted to a list and then assigned to our file list place holder. The next line prints each item in the list, i. e., prints all the files in */Users/.../temp* directory.

Now, let's analyze the second method, *printListOfSubDirectories*. The place holder, in this case, is a list of strings. The filter method checks if an item is a directory. If it is a directory, then it maps to its *getName* method. The collection is, finally, converted to the place holder list, *listOfSubDirectories*. The last statement prints each element of the place holder.

Next, let's discuss system commands. Scala allows us to execute operating system commands from the program itself; Scala was designed to scale from simple scripting to complex programs. This ability to have control over processes gives programmers the ability to manipulate system level processes.

```scala
import scala.io.Source
import scala.sys.process._
object SystemCommand {
   def main(args: Array[String]): Unit = {
      val lsCommand = Process("ls").lineStream
      lsCommand foreach println

      val htmlContents = "curl https://www.scala-lang.org".!
      println(htmlContents)

      val html =
               Source.fromURL("https://www.scala-lang.org").
               mkString
      println(html)
   }
}
```

Fig. 6.7: System Commands

Figure 6.7 presents several approaches. The first approach creates a *Process* object by passing a system command as a parameter. The result is stream of lines, which can be printed using *foreach*. The second approach is to have the system command within double quotes and then call an exclamation method. In our example, it crawls to `https://www.scala-lang.org` and gets html content, which is then assigned to *htmlContents*. Alternatively, we can also use *fromURL* method of *scala.io.Source* class, as shown in the program.

So there are different ways of doing the same thing, which is good. Based on your preference, you could pick one over another. For example, if you are not comfortable with Shell scripts, you can use alternative Scala APIs, as shown in this program. Some developers like OS commands as they get to use all the features of OS level scripting. In any case, you can do the job. That's why Scala provides multiple options.

6.7 Conclusion

In this chapter, we discussed regular expressions. Regular expressions give us more power to process strings. If string APIs do not provide the functionality that we are looking for, then we go for regular expressions. Next, we demonstrated single character input and single character output, with the help of complete programs. Single character processing is important in many areas, including those that have limited memory and transmission power. Next, we covered reading from and writing to a file. These are handy operations in many applications, including big data. Finally, we covered directory navigation, including system commands.

6.8 Review Questions

1. If we define *phone* as """"(\d+)(-)(\d+)(-)(\d+) """".r, *data* as 444443 555-555-5555 4455 3-4-4, and command as *phone findFirstIn data*, what is the output in the Scala interpreter?
2. For the same pattern and data as in Problem # 1, what is the output for command *phone.findAllIn(data).toArray*?
3. For the same pattern and data as in Problem #1, what is the output for command *phone.findAllIn(data).toList*?
4. Let's define *digit* as """"(\d+) """".r, *data* as *Google 45 is 90 *search! engine*, and command as *digit.findAllIn(data).toArray*, what is the output?
5. When do we need single character processing?
6. When is flat file processing applicable?
7. What is the importance of *scala.io.Source*?

6.9 Problems

1. Write a program to read individual characters from a text file.

2. Write a program to read html contents from `https://www.scala-lang.org` and store this content in a text file. Display the size of this file on the console.
3. Read the contents of the file produced by the program for Problem #2 and find the total occurrence of word *Scala*.
4. Browse the website of *The Guardian*, `https://www.theguardian.com/world`. Please note the response time, qualitatively; it is pretty fast compared with *CNN*, `http://www.cnn.com/`. This site was implemented using the Scala based framework, Play (as of 2017). Let's assume there is a competition for these two sites and the winner is determined by the occurrence of the word "news" on the home page, i.e., the higher the occurrence, the higher will be the score. Now, write a program that reads the contents, performs the necessary analysis, and decides the winner. Print the name and count for both the websites and display the winner, on the console.

6.10 Answers to Review Questions

1. Option[String] = Some(555-555-5555)
2. Array[String] = Array(555-555-5555, 3-4-4)
3. List[String] = List(555-555-5555, 3-4-4)
4. Array[String] = Array(45, 90)
5. When we need character level control, we need single character processing. Also single character processing becomes important when there is limited available memory and/or limited transmission bandwidth.
6. Flat file processing is applicable when we use flat files as a persistence system, instead of databases. In some cases, flat files may be used together with databases to provide additional capabilities.
7. One of the applications of *scala.io.Source* is that we can create flat file data sources.

6.11 Solutions to Problems

1.
```scala
import java.io.{IOException, FileNotFoundException}
import scala.io.Source
object ReadCharsFromTextFile {
    def main(args: Array[String]): Unit = {
        val fileName = "/Users/.../temp/InputFile.txt"
        var source: scala.io.BufferedSource = null
        try {
            source = Source.fromFile(fileName)
            for(char <- source) {
                println(char)
            }
        } catch {
          case e: FileNotFoundException =>
           println("File not found.")
          case e: IOException => println("IO Problem.")
          case e: Exception => println("Something went wrong.")
        } finally {
          source.close()
        }
    }
}
```

2.
```scala
import java.io.{File, PrintWriter}
import scala.io.Source
object ReadFromURL {
    def main(args: Array[String]): Unit = {
        val outFileName = "/Users/.../temp/ScalaFile.txt"
        val html =
                Source.fromURL("https://www.scala-lang.org").
                 mkString
        writeToFile(outFileName, html)
        val scalaFile =
                new File("/Users/.../temp/ScalaFile.txt")
        val fileSize = scalaFile.length
        println("The size of the file written is "+
         fileSize+" KB")
    }

    def writeToFile(fileName: String, content: String): Unit = {
        var printWriter: PrintWriter = null
        try {
           printWriter = new PrintWriter(new File(fileName))
           printWriter.write(content)
        } catch {
           case e: Exception => println("Something went wrong.")
        } finally {
           printWriter.close()
        }
    }
}
```

3.
```scala
import java.io.{IOException, FileNotFoundException}
import scala.io.Source
object ReadFromHtmlTextFile {
   def main(args: Array[String]): Unit = {
      val fileName = "/Users/.../temp/ScalaFile.txt"
      var source: scala.io.BufferedSource = null
      try {
         source = Source.fromFile(fileName)
         val allTokens = source.mkString.split("\\s+")
         var count = 0
         for(token <- allTokens) {
            token match {
               case "Scala" => count += 1
               case _ => count += 0
            }
         }
         println("Total count for word Scala: "+count)
      } catch {
         case e: FileNotFoundException =>
          println("File not found.")
         case e: IOException => println("IO problem.")
         case e: Exception => println("Something went wrong.")
      } finally {
         source.close()
      }
   }
}
```

4.
```scala
import scala.io.{BufferedSource, Source}
object CNNVsTheGuardian {
    def main(args: Array[String]): Unit = {
        computeNewsWinner
    }

    def computeNewsWinner: Unit = {
        var cnnHtmlSource: BufferedSource  = null
        var theGuardianHtmlSource: BufferedSource  = null
        try {
            cnnHtmlSource = Source.fromURL("http://www.cnn.com/")
            theGuardianHtmlSource =
             Source.fromURL("https://www.theguardian.com/us")
            val cnnAllTokens = cnnHtmlSource.
             mkString.split("\\s+")
            val theGuardianAllTokens =
                    theGuardianHtmlSource.mkString.split("\\s+")
            var cnnCount = 0
            for (token <- cnnAllTokens) {
                token match {
                    case "news" => cnnCount += 1
                    case _ => cnnCount += 0
                }
            }
            var guardianCount = 0
            for (token <- theGuardianAllTokens) {
                token match {
                    case "news" => guardianCount += 1
                    case _ => guardianCount += 0
                }
            }
            var winnerMessage = ""
            if (cnnCount > guardianCount) {
                winnerMessage = "CNN is the winner."
            } else {
                winnerMessage = "The Guardian is the winner"
            }
            println(winnerMessage)
            println("CNN Score: " + cnnCount)
            println("The Guardian Score: " + guardianCount)
        } catch {
            case e: Exception => println("Something went wrong.")
        }
    }
}
```

Chapter 7
Inheritance and Composition

There are numerous natural hierarchies in the real world. Also we, human beings, have created many systems that have hierarchies. In hierarchies, sometimes things flow from top to bottom, and at some other times, things propagate from bottom to top. Depending upon domains, these things can be properties, behavior, instructions, etc. When we write programs to solve problems related to hierarchies, it is natural to model real world hierarchies with some programming features. In this way, it is convenient to relate programs to the original problem. Also it is much easier to maintain the programs and hence reduces cost over a period of time. Scala provides features to represent hierarchies. Also it provides features to combine things, which maps to syntheses or compositions, in the real world.

Inheritance is a mechanism by which one entity can get resources from another entity; it can be used to model *is-a* relationships. In the real world, one entity can inherit from multiple other entities. It is also true that multiple entities can inherit from a single entity. Scala supports these real world scenarios through classes, inheritance, composition, and traits. Further, inheritance is like a parent–child relationship. One of the major advantages of inheritance is that it maintains the original relationship and promotes code reuse.

Composition is a mechanism to combine multiple entities to form a larger entity; it can be used to model *has-a* relationships. For example, a car is composed of numerous parts. If we try to model a car, we might end up with a *Car* class and many other classes related to parts, which can become fields of the *Car* class. For example, there can be a *Wheel* class to represent wheels. Since wheels are parts of a car, they can be combined with other classes that are parts of a car too. The whole combination, *Car* class, represents a real world car.

7.1 Extending Classes

A class can inherit all non-private members from another class by using the reserved word *extends*. When a class *A* extends class *B*, the type of class *A*, which is *A*,

© Springer International Publishing AG 2017
B.P. Upadhyaya, *Programming with Scala*, Undergraduate
Topics in Computer Science, https://doi.org/10.1007/978-3-319-69368-2_7

becomes a sub-type of the type of class *B*, which is *B*. Figure 7.1 shows one super class *Vehicle* and two sub classes—*Car* and *Truck*.

```
class Vehicle(make: String, model: String, year: Int) {
    def calculatePrice(varFactor: Int): Double = {
        val price = ((year - 2000) * varFactor) * 1000
        price
    }
}

class Car(make: String,
          model: String,
          year: Int,
          mode: String) extends
        Vehicle(make, model, year) {
    // Car specific methods here
}

class Truck(make: String,
            model: String,
            year: Int,
            operation: String) extends
        Vehicle(make, model, year) {
    // Truck specific methods here
}
```

Fig. 7.1: Extending a Class

The class *Vehicle* is a super class that has a common method called *calculatePrice*, which is inherited by sub classes *Car* and *Truck*. Please do not worry about the correctness of the formula, because the focus, here, is on inheriting the class members. Also price is calculated differently by different manufacturers. Please note that the class *Vehicle* has a constructor defined in the same line, with three parameters. Similarly, each of the sub classes has a constructor defined in the same line to that of the class declaration. The sub class *Car* has an additional constructor argument called *mode* and the sub class *Truck* has an additional constructor parameter called *operation*.

The purpose of the constructor argument *mode*, in *Car*, is to represent whether a car is for personal use or for public transportation. Similarly, the constructor argument, *operation*, in *Truck*, is to model whether a truck is operated for shipping or for farming. Please note that three parameters are passed to the super class constructor while declaring sub classes. This is a feature that Scala provides, you don't have to write a separate statement to pass parameters to the super class constructor. Please note that a class can directly inherit from only one class using the reserved word *extends*. When we need to model real world multiple inheritance scenarios, we can use traits, which will be discussed in Chapter 8.

7.2 Overriding Methods and Fields

Overriding is a feature that allows programmers to re-define a behavior or a state in sub classes. Scala allows a method to be overridden by a method or a field. Figure 7.2 has two classes—a class called *Shape* and another class called *Rectangle*. Area is a common property for different types of shapes; it has been defined as a method in the *Shape* class. Also this class has another method called *message* that is supposed to print what kind of shape the current object is.

```
class Shape(name: String) {
   def area: Double = 0.0
   def message = println("This is "+name)
   val numOfDimensions = 0
}

class Rectangle(name: String,
               length: Double,
               breadth: Double) extends
     Shape(name) {
   override def area: Double  = length * breadth
   override val numOfDimensions = 2
}
```

Fig. 7.2: Overriding a Method

The class rectangle inherits both *area* and *message* methods of the class *Shape*. Please note that these are methods without parameters; they look like variables or values. If the reserved word *def* comes before an identifier, then that is a method; values are defined using the reserved word *val* and variables are defined using the reserved word *var*. Also the sub class inherits the field *numOfDimensions*, as it is a non-private member.

The class *Rectangle* overrides the behavior of the method *area*. In *Shape* class, it is assigned value 0.0, whereas in *Rectangle* class, it is calculated based on values coming from constructor parameters *length* and *breadth*. So the method of computation has changed in the sub class. Similarly, the field *numOfDimensions* has been redefined in the sub class, by assigning it a different value. Please note that re-assignment to a *val* is not allowed in the same class, but it can be overridden using the reserved word, *override*.

7.3 Abstract Classes

Abstract classes are those classes that do not have implementations for all of their methods. Sometimes, we need to defer the implementation to sub classes; that's when we use abstract classes. Classes can be declared as abstract by using a modifier *abstract*, as shown in Figure 7.3.

```
abstract class BankAccount(custName: String,
                           accNumber: Int,
                           accType: String,
                           principal: Double) {
   def calculateAmount(timeInYears: Double): Double
}

class CheckingAccount(custName: String,
                      accNumber: Int,
                      accType: String,
                      principal: Double,
                      interestRate: Double) extends
              BankAccount(custName,
                          accNumber,
                          accType,
                          principal) {
   override def calculateAmount(duration: Double): Double = {
      val totalAmount =
       principal * (1 + (interestRate * duration))
      totalAmount
   }
}
```

Fig. 7.3: Abstract Class

The class *BankAccount* is an abstract class and hence the method *calculateAmount* does not have an implementation. If the class is not declared *abstract*, we get a compile time error. The class *CheckingAccount* extends *BankAccount* and hence should either implement the inherited abstract method or declare itself as an abstract class. Please note that the method does not require the modifier *abstract*. It is automatically inferred, if the method does not have a body.

7.4 Invoking Super Class Constructors

Invoking a superclass constructor is fairly straight-forward. In fact, we have already seen several examples. When a class extends another class, the reserved word *extends* is followed by a class name, which becomes a superclass. We can call a superclass constructor by passing parameters in the parentheses as shown in Figure 7.3.

Just to be clear, let's say there are two classes—*A* and *B*. Further let's assume *A* has two constructor parameters and *B* has three constructor parameters, as shown below. Please note how parameters *x* and *y* are being passed to *A*; this is superclass constructor invoking.

```
class A(a: Int, b: Int) {
   // Code here
}

class B(x: Int, y: Int, z: Int) extends A(x,y) {
   // Code here
}
```

7.5 Polymorphism and Dynamic Binding

The literal meaning of polymorphism is many forms. In chemistry, we have substances that crystallize into two or more chemically identical but crystallographically distinct forms. Similarly, animals make sounds but these sounds are different. Figure 7.4 demonstrates a program that models animal sounds using Scala's polymorphism and dynamic binding.

The class *Animal* is a super class to classes *Cat*, *Cow*, and *Duck*. Each of these sub classes have overridden the super class method *makeSound*. In the singleton object *AnimalSoundApp*, we have the *makeAnimalSound* method that has *Animal* as a parameter. In the body of this method, it invokes the *makeSound* method on the object *animal*, which is of type *Animal*.

When we run this program, it does not print "Abstract sound" four times. In fact, it prints the sound from each of the four classes. How does this happen? Even though the type of *animal* is *Animal*, the binding happens during run time. So if we create an object of type *Cat* and pass it to the method *makeAnimalSound*, then *makeSound* of type *Cat* is invoked. This is happening because of dynamic binding and polymorphism. We have different forms of *makeSound* in the superclass and its sub classes.

```
class Animal(name: String) {
   def makeSound(): Unit = {
      println(name+" : Abstract sound")
   }
}

class Cat(name: String) extends Animal(name) {
   override def makeSound(): Unit = {
      println(name+" : Meow")
   }
}

class Cow(name: String) extends Animal(name) {
   override def makeSound(): Unit = {
      println(name+ " : Moo")
   }
}

class Duck(name: String) extends Animal(name) {
   override def makeSound(): Unit = {
      println(name+" : Quack")
   }
}

object AnimalSoundApp {
   def main(args: Array[String]): Unit = {
      makeAnimalSound(new Animal("Abstract"))
      makeAnimalSound(new Cat("Cat"))
      makeAnimalSound(new Cow("Cow"))
      makeAnimalSound(new Duck("Duck"))
   }
   def makeAnimalSound(animal: Animal): Unit = {
      animal.makeSound()
   }
}
```

Fig. 7.4: Polymorphism and Dynamic Binding

7.6 Composition

Like inheritance, composition is a mechanism that allows one class to get features from another class. Unlike inheritance, composition satisfies a *has-a* relationship. This is more like a *whole-part* relationship. For example, if we would like to model a university, then we can have a *University* class. One of the building blocks of a university is a department; so we can have a *Department* class.

Figure 7.5 shows two classes—*University* and *Department*. The university class has two fields, one for a biology department and one for a computer department. The type for both of these departments is *Department*. So we can say that a university has departments; in this case, it has a biology department and a computer department.

```
class University(name: String) {
    val biologyDept = new Department("Biology")
    val computerDept = new Department("Computer")
    // Code here
}

class Department(name: String) {
    var speciality: String = null
    var size: Int = 0
    def registerStudentForCourse(name: String): Unit = {
        // Code here
    }
}
```

Fig. 7.5: Composition

The *Department* is a regular class and has two field variables, *speciality* and *size*, and a method called *registerStudentForCourse*. Please note that this class does not extend *University* class, because a department is not a type of university, rather it is a part of a university. Sometimes, parts can get some state related attributes and some behaviors from the whole. In that case, we can group such common items in a feature called *trait*, which will be discussed in Chapter 8.

7.7 Conclusion

In this chapter, we discussed inheritance and composition. Inheritance models *is-a* relationships and composition models *has-a* relationships. We discussed how to extend classes so that non-private members can be re-used. Sometimes, we need to change the imported state and behavior. For that, Scala provides method overriding and field overriding. Next, we discussed abstract classes and demonstrated how to call super class constructors. We wrote a complete program for polymorphism and dynamic binding. Finally, we discussed composition, sometimes known as a *whole-part* relationship.

7.8 Review Questions

1. What is the major difference between inheritance and composition?
2. When do we use the reserved word *extends*?
3. What is overriding?
4. Can we override fields?
5. When do we use abstract classes?
6. What is polymorphism and what is its application?

7. When do we use composition?

7.9 Problems

1. For the program in Figure 7.1, write code for a singleton object, with a main method, which instantiates three classes. Then invoke the method *calculatePrice* of each of those instances, and print the results on the console.
2. For the program in Figure 7.2 , write the necessary code to instantiate the *Rectangle* class and invoke all of its methods.
3. Using the classes in Figure 7.3, find the total amount for: principal = USD 74,000.00, interest rate = 5%, and duration = 3 years and 6 months. Print the result on the console.

7.10 Answers to Review Questions

1. The major difference between inheritance and composition is that inheritance is a *is-a* relationship, whereas composition is a *has-a* relationship.
2. We use the reserved word *extends* when we need to inherit members of a class.
3. Overriding is a feature that allows us to redefine fields and methods in a sub class.
4. Yes, we can override fields.
5. We use abstract classes when we need to defer some of the implementation to sub classes.
6. Polymorphism is a feature which allows the same name but different behavior. One of the methods to implement it is dynamic binding.
7. We use composition when we need to model *has-a* or *whole-part* relationships.

7.11 Solutions to Problems

```
1. object VehicleApp {
      def main(args: Array[String]): Unit = {
         val vehicle = new Vehicle("Rolls-Royce", "Phantom", 2015)
         val car = new Car("Toyota", "Rav4", 2006, "Personal")
         val truck = new Truck("Ford", "Raptor", 2017, "Farm")
         println(vehicle.calculatePrice(2))
         println(car.calculatePrice(4))
         println(truck.calculatePrice(3))
      }
   }
```

```scala
2. object ShapeApp {
     def main(args: Array[String]): Unit = {
       val rect = new Rectangle("Rectangle", 2.0, 4.0)
       println(rect.message)
       println(rect.area)
     }
   }

3. object BankAccountApp {
     def main(args: Array[String]): Unit = {
       val checkingAccount =
        new CheckingAccount("James Janowski",
           12345, "Checking", 740000.00,0.05)
       println(checkingAccount.calculateAmount(3.5))
     }
   }
```

Chapter 8
Traits

In the real world, we have different ways to interact with things. Most of the time, we can find some sort of interface for interaction. Also most human made things have interfaces. For example, if we are driving a car, we interact with the dashboard, steering being a part of it. All of these interfaces represent certain kinds of attributes. Sometimes, it is convenient to classify these attributes and model attributes as well as entities as classes. Sometimes, it is convenient to group attributes and mix them as needed to form a new entity that represents part of a computational problem. This is when traits come into the picture.

8.1 Traits as Interfaces

Traits can be used as interfaces. If we have many classes forming a module, then we can expose the members through traits. Figure 8.1 shows how to use a trait. First we define a trait called *Socializable*, which has a single method *interact*. A class can implement a trait using the keywords *extends* or *with*. If we are implementing only one trait, then we must use *extends*. If we are implementing multiple traits, the first one must use *extends* and the remaining ones must use *with*; there cannot be two *extends*.

In Figure 8.1, the classes *Adult* and *Child* implement the trait *Socializable*. Each of these classes has a body for the method *interact*. This scenario is similar to inheriting from an abstract class. We could make the trait *Socializable* an abstract class and the rest of the code would work fine, as far as the syntax is concerned. But there is one major modeling problem with this, i.e., *Socializable* is not a natural hierarchy for *Adult* and *Child*. It is more of an attribute.

One might ask, why don't we make *Socializable* an attribute of *Adult* and *Child*? In terms of modeling, that is a good representation. Since *Socializable* has a method, it should appear as a class somewhere so that we can make it a part of *Adult* and *Child* through composition. But *Socializable* is not an entity and hence not a good candidate for a class. What is the best thing to do? It would be better as a trait.

© Springer International Publishing AG 2017
B.P. Upadhyaya, *Programming with Scala*, Undergraduate
Topics in Computer Science, https://doi.org/10.1007/978-3-319-69368-2_8

```
trait Socializable {
   def interact()
}

class Adult extends Socializable {
   def interact(): Unit = {
      println("Interact")
   }
}

class Child extends Socializable {
   def interact(): Unit = {
      println("Play")
   }
}
```

Fig. 8.1: Trait as an Interface

8.2 Construction Order and Linearizing

Traits have constructors, but the parameters are not passed using parentheses, like in a class constructor. Statements in the body of a trait are parts of the trait constructor. Trait constructors are invoked after the super class constructors and before the class constructor. Trait constructors are executed from left to right, i.e., the one on the left is executed first and so on; the right-most trait constructor is the last one to be executed. Also the parent constructor is executed before the trait constructor is executed. A trait can extend a class as well as a trait. The use of reserved words *extends* and *with* is the same as in a class definition or in a class declaration. In the case of a shared parent, it is evaluated only once.

Let's look at Figure 8.2 and examine the rules. We have four traits—*Friendly*, *Climbing*, *Agile*, and *Powerful*. Similarly, we have three abstract classes—*Carnivore*, *Felis*, and *Panthera* and two concrete classes—*Cat* and *Lion*. The abstract class *Felis* extends another abstract class *Carnivora*, in accordance with the conventional classification presented in Table 1.1, page 2. Similarly, class *Panthera* inherits from class *Carnivora*.

The class *Cat* inherits from class *Felis* and implements traits *Agile*, *Climbing*, and *Friendly*. The class *Lion* inherits from class *Panthera* and implements trait *Powerful*. The modeling should be intuitive. Now, if write a singleton object with necessary code to invoke method *befriend* of instance of type *Cat*, we get the following output, which complies with the rules discussed earlier.

```
Abstract class Carnivore: I am a carnivore.
Abstract class Felis: I am Small
Trait Agile: I am agile.
Trait Climbing: I can climb.
Trait Friendly: I am friendly.
Cat: I can befriend.
```

```
trait Friendly {
   println("Trait Friendly: I am friendly.")
   def befriend()
}
trait Climbing {
   println("Trait Climbing: I can climb.")
   def climb()
}
trait Agile {
   println("Trait Agile: I am agile.")
   def moveQuick()
}
trait Powerful {
   println("Trait Powerful: I am powerful.")
   def fight()
}
abstract class Carnivore(name: String) {
   println("Abstract class Carnivore: I am a carnivore.")
   def eatMeat()
}
abstract class Felis(name: String) extends Carnivore(name){
   println("Abstract class Felis: I am "+size)
   def size = "Small"
}
abstract class Panthera(name: String) extends Carnivore(name){
   def size = "Big"
   println("Abstract class Panthera: I am "+size)
}
class Cat(name: String) extends Felis(name)
   with Agile with Climbing with Friendly {
   def befriend(): Unit = {println("Cat: I can befriend.")}
   def eatMeat(): Unit  = {println("Cat: I eat meat.")}
   def climb(): Unit = {println("Cat: I can climb.")}
   def moveQuick(): Unit = {println("I can move quickly.")}
}
class Lion(name: String) extends Panthera(name) with Powerful {
   def eatMeat() = {println("Lion: I eat meat.")}
   def fight(): Unit = {println("Lion: I can fight and win.")}
}
```

Fig. 8.2: Construction Order and Linearizing

How does Scala handle the mix of traits, abstract classes, and classes? It does something called *linearization*. The mixing of classes and objects is called *mix-in*. The linearization gives us a technical specification of all super types of a type. One more rule to remember: the order in which constructors are executed is the reverse of the linearization. Linearization is defined as:

If A *extends* B *with* C *with* ... *with* Z, then $linear(A) = A \rhd linear(Z) \rhd ... linear(C) \rhd linear(B)$, where $linear(x)$ is the linearization of x and $\rhd$ is "concatenation and duplication removal, with the right overriding the left".

Now, let's analyze *Cat extends Felis with Agile with Climbing with Friendly.*
linear(Cat)
$\Rightarrow Cat \triangleright linear(Friendly) \triangleright linear(Climbing) \triangleright linear(Agile) \triangleright linear(Felis)$
$\Rightarrow Cat \triangleright (Friendly \triangleright AnyRef \triangleright Any) \triangleright (Climbing \triangleright AnyRef \triangleright Any) \triangleright (Agile \triangleright AnyRef \triangleright Any) \triangleright (Felis \triangleright (Carnivore \triangleright AnyRef \triangleright Any))$
$\Rightarrow Cat \triangleright Friendly \triangleright Climbing \triangleright Agile \triangleright Felis \triangleright Carnivore \triangleright AnyRef \triangleright Any$

The constructor invocation order is *Any, AnyRef, Carnivore, Felis, Agile, Climbing, Friendly*, and *Cat*. For the custom written mix-in, the constructor invocation order is *Carnivore, Felis, Agile, Climbing, Friendly*, and *Cat*.

8.3 Trait Members

A trait can have fields and methods, as well as blocks. Blocks should be assigned to a *val* or to a *var*. A field can be of custom defined type, as shown below. The custom defined type can be an abstract class or a concrete class. The statements that are not method definitions are parts of the trait constructor.

```
trait TraitExperiments {
    val length = 5
    var breadth: Int
    def area()
    def sumOfLenBreadth(customLength: Int) =
     customLength + breadth
    val experiment: TraitExp
    val output = {
        println(length)
        println(breadth)
    }
}

abstract class TraitExp {
    def expMethod()
}
```

In the definition above, *length* is defined as value 5. *breadth* is declared as a variable and can be overridden later. Similarly, the method *area* is an abstract method and can be implemented by a class that inherits from this trait. *experiment* is a variable of type *TraitExp* and should be overridden later by a class inheriting from this trait; a trait that inherits from this trait does not have to implement.

The identifier *output* does not have any interesting value assigned to it. If we write the necessary code to implement the trait *TraitExperiments* and invoke *output*, we get a message printed. So it is up to us, the programmers, to provide the correct meanings to the programming elements. The syntax of the language is flexible enough to enable a wide variety of combinations, but this flexibility should be used meaningfully.

8.4 Multiple Inheritance

It is common to encounter a multiple inheritance scenario in the real world. For example, we have departments in universities. The Department of Biology is a traditional department; this is somewhat true for the Department of Computer Science as well. But the Department of Computational Biology is relatively new. If we are developing a program to keep track of activities in all the departments then we need to model correctly. *Department*, *Biology*, *Computer*, *ComputationalBiology*, and *BiologicalComputation*, all are good candidates for class names. If we model all of them as classes, it can form a diamond inheritance with ambiguity. Further we cannot get properties of both *Biology* and *Computer*, because *Biology* does not extend *Computer* naturally and vice-versa.

```scala
trait Department {
    val name = "Department"
}

trait Biology extends Department {
    override val name = "Biology"
}

trait Computer extends Department {
    override val name = "Computer"
}

class ComputationalBiology extends Biology with Computer

class BiologicalComputation extends Computer with Biology

object DepartmentApp {
    def main(args: Array[String]): Unit = {
        val compBio = new ComputationalBiology
        println(compBio.name)
        val bioComp = new BiologicalComputation
        println(bioComp.name)
    }
}
```

Fig. 8.3: Multiple Inheritance

Scala allows us to model this kind of scenario effectively using traits. Figure 8.3 shows a solution for a typical diamond inheritance. Scala forces us to override the common members, which resolves ambiguity. Further, the order in which traits appear in a class definition also determines the overriding. The classes *Computation-alBiology* and *BiologicalComputation* have a different order for traits and hence different outcomes. The first *println* prints "Computer", whereas the second *println* prints "Biology". Remember, for traits, the order of constructor invocation is left to right.

8.5 Traits with Implementations

Traits can have all abstract members, or some abstract members and some concrete members, or all concrete members. Figure 8.4 shows traits with different levels of implementation. The trait *Teaching* has two abstract fields—*courseName* and *credit*. The method *teach* has implementation, whereas the method *writeBook* is an abstract method. Similarly, the trait *Researching* has two abstract fields—*researchArea* and *durationInMonth*. Further, it has one method *research*, which is abstract. So the trait *Teaching* is richer than the trait *Researching*. Traits with less implementation are also known as thinner traits.

The class *Professor* inherits from both the traits and is a concrete class; hence it is required to implement all the abstract members; field members are assigned values and methods are assigned corresponding implementations. Finally, we have the singleton object *TeachingApp*, which creates an instance of the class *Professor* and invokes its *teach* method, which has its definition in the trait *Teaching*.

```scala
trait Teaching {
    val courseName: String
    val credit: Int
    def teach() = {
       println("Teaching")
       // Code here
    }
    def writeBook()
}

trait Researching {
    val researchArea: String
    val durationInMonth: Int
    def research()
}

class Professor(name: String) extends
 Teaching with Researching {
    val courseName = "Scala"
    val credit = 3
    def writeBook() = {
       println("Book")
       // Code here
    }
    val researchArea = "Language Technology"
    val durationInMonth = 6
    def research() = {
       println("Research")
       // Code here
    }
}

object TeachingApp {
    def main(args: Array[String]): Unit = {
       val prof = new Professor("Charles Darwin")
       println(prof.teach())
    }
}
```

Fig. 8.4: Traits with Implementation

8.6 Conclusion

First we saw how traits can be used to model real world interfaces. Then we discussed the construction order of traits along with classes. The construction order is an important element as it determines the order of execution of mix-in. Linearization helps us to understand how Scala builds the order to execution when there are many traits and classes. Also we covered trait members and how Scala helps us to model multiple inheritance. Finally, we discussed traits with implementations; traits that have implementation are like abstract classes.

8.7 Review Questions

1. In terms of inheritance, what is the major difference between an abstract class and a trait?
2. If a class extends from another class and implements two traits, what is the construction invocation order?
3. Can we implement a method in a trait?
4. What Scala feature helps us to model real world multiple inheritance?
5. For the following code snippet, what is the output for *c.isInstanceOf[A]*, *c.isInstanceOf[B]*, and *c.isInstanceOf[C]*?

```scala
scala> trait A
scala> trait B extends A
scala> class C extends B with A
```

6. What is the output when the following program is executed?

```scala
trait A {
   print("A")
}
trait B extends A {
   print("B")
}
class C extends B with A {
   print("C")
}
object TraitApp {
   def main(args: Array[String]): Unit = {
      val c = new C
   }
}
```

7. What is the output when the following program is executed?

```scala
trait A {
   print("A")
}
trait B extends A {
   print("B")
}
class C extends A with B {
   print("C")
}
object TraitApp {
   def main(args: Array[String]): Unit = {
      val c = new C
   }
}
```

8. What is the output when the following program is executed?

```
trait A {
    print("A")
}
trait B {
    print("B")
}
class C extends B with A {
    print("C")
}
object TraitApp {
    def main(args: Array[String]): Unit = {
        val c = new C
    }
}
```

9. What is the output when the following program is executed?

```
trait A {
    print("A")
}
trait B {
    print("B")
}
class C extends A with B {
    print("C")
}
object TraitApp {
    def main(args: Array[String]): Unit = {
        val c = new C
    }
}
```

8.8 Problems

1. For the program in Figure 8.2, write necessary code to invoke the method *be-friend*.
2. Using traits, write a program to calculate the area of two-dimensional objects with edges. You can limit your code to rectangles and triangles for this exercise.
3. Write a mix-in to calculate the salaries of a full professor and of an assistant professor. Make realistic assumptions whenever required. Also make the program as re-usable as possible.

8.9 Answers to Review Questions

1. In terms of inheritance, the major difference between an abstract class and a trait is that we cannot directly inherit from more than one abstract class, but we can directly inherit from more than one trait.
2. The construction invocation order is: super class, traits left to right, and this class.
3. Yes, we can implement a method in a trait. In that case, it becomes a rich interface.
4. Traits help us to model real world multiple inheritance. We can combine traits with abstract classes as well as with concrete classes, to model real world multiple inheritance.
5. true, true, and true.
6. ABC
7. ABC
8. BAC
9. ABC

8.10 Solutions to Problems

1.
```scala
object TraitsConstructorOrderApp {
  def main(args: Array[String]): Unit = {
    val cat = new Cat("Ramse")
    println(cat.befriend())
  }
}
```

2.
```scala
trait Rectangular {
    val length: Double
    val breadth: Double
    def area(): Double = length * breadth
}

trait Triangular {
    val base: Double
    val height: Double
    def area(): Double = 0.5 * (base * height)
}

class MyRectangle(len: Double, bre: Double) {
    val length = len
    val breadth = bre
}

class MyTriangle(bas: Double, hei: Double) {
    val base = bas
    val height = hei
}

object AreaApp {
    def main(args: Array[String]): Unit = {
        println((new MyRectangle(2,4) with Rectangular).area())
        println((new MyTriangle(2,4) with Triangular).area())
    }
}
```

3.
```scala
trait Teaching {
    val grade: Int
    val salaryInUSD: Double
    def monthlySalaryInUSD = salaryInUSD + (grade * 10)
}

trait Researching {
    val grade: Int
    val compensationInUSD: Double
    def monthlyCompInUSD = compensationInUSD + (grade * 2)
}

class Professor(name: String) extends
 Teaching with Researching {
    val grade = 10
    val salaryInUSD = 12000.00
    val compensationInUSD = 3000.00
}

class AsstProfessor(name: String) extends Professor(name) {
    override val grade = 5
    override val salaryInUSD = 8000.00
    override val compensationInUSD = 4000.00
}

object ProfSalaryApp {
    def main(args: Array[String]): Unit = {
       val prof = new Professor("Darwin")
       println(prof.monthlyCompInUSD + prof.monthlySalaryInUSD)
       val asstProf = new AsstProfessor("Newton")
       println(asstProf.monthlyCompInUSD+
        asstProf.monthlySalaryInUSD)
    }
}
```

Chapter 9
Functions

Functions date back several centuries and are some of the most widely used techniques in mathematics [Hod05] [Dur88][Dur89a][Dur89b]. They provide rigorous methods for analysis and inference. The history of mathematics shows that functions were used to express thought [Boo05] [Hod05]. This is very well aligned with computer programming. You might have already realized that we express our thought when we program; we tell a computer what to do, with the help of a language that the computer understands and we, human beings, understand. Remember the definition of *computing* and *computation* from Chapter1. In each chapter, we are doing either computing, or computation, or both.

Now coming closer to Scala programming, let's remember functions from our mathematics lessons. We might ask ourselves: *Where did we use functions? What computational goals were achieved? Could we do without functions?*. Most likely, our answers will converge to a common point: *functions are necessary tools*. Functions were developed to solve complex computational problems and they help us to express our thought, in the form of solutions or solutions steps. The Scala programming language provides features to encode our solutions or solutions steps, in a machine understandable form so that we can achieve our computational goals. In this chapter, we discuss different aspects of Scala functions.

In previous chapters, we discussed mostly object oriented programming although functional aspects were involved. Now, we add one of the major features from the functional programming paradigm, i.e., functions as first class citizens. In Scala, functions can be treated as values, discussed in detail later in this chapter. Since Scala is both an object oriented and a functional programming language, we can mix objects with functions and vice-versa. One of the advantages of using Scala is that we don't have to switch programming languages, in order to program in different paradigms.

Based on our needs, we can mix different features that Scala provides. Not only that, if we think we don't have sufficient features to meet our needs, we can extend the language; Scala was designed to be extended. We will see, later in this chapter, how convenient it is to create our own control structures. This is one of the advantages of functional programming. And don't forget, we can do all this without

© Springer International Publishing AG 2017
B.P. Upadhyaya, *Programming with Scala*, Undergraduate
Topics in Computer Science, https://doi.org/10.1007/978-3-319-69368-2_9

changing the programming language. You will soon see one of the major advantages of using the Scala programming language.

9.1 Functions as Methods

Functions can be used as as methods, by defining them as a member of an object. We have presented numerous examples in previous chapters. Just as a refresher, Figure 9.1 presents two objects: *SomeObjects* and *SomeObjectsApp*. *SomeObjectsApp* has a main method that invokes the public method *calculateArea* in *SomeObjects*.

```scala
object SomeObjects {
    def calculateArea(objType: String, dim: Int*): Double = {
        if(objType.equals("Rectangle")) {
            rectangleArea(dim(0), dim(1))
        } else if(objType.equals("Square")){
            squareArea(dim(0))
        } else {
            0
        }
    }

    private def rectangleArea(length: Double,
     breadth: Double): Double = {
        length * breadth
    }

    private def squareArea(dimension: Double): Double = {
        dimension * dimension
    }
}
object SomeObjectsApp {
    def main(args: Array[String]): Unit = {
        println(SomeObjects.calculateArea("Rectangle",3,2))
        println(SomeObjects.calculateArea("Square",3))
    }
}
```

Fig. 9.1: Functions as Methods

Since singleton objects have only only instance, member methods are more like functions. In other words, this is a typical implementation of functions as methods. Two private methods *rectangleArea* and *squareArea* are not visible from *SomeObjectsApp*. These methods are internally used by the public method *calculateArea*, to calculate the area of respective real world objects. *dim: Int** means zero or more integer values. It is to take care of different types of objects that have different dimensional elements like length, breadth, height, etc.

In this program, *calculateArea* is a common method that can be used to calculate the area of rectangles and squares. This is a generalized code, one of the attributes discussed in Section 1.5, page 12. By adding one more if-else block we can cover circles as well.

9.2 Anonymous Functions

It is not necessary to provide a name for a function. This is a handy feature when we have a small algorithm to apply. For example, if we have an array containing all prime numbers smaller than 10 and would like to calculate the square of those numbers, we can pass pass the squaring function to another function or to another method, as shown below.

```
scala> List(1, 2, 3, 5, 7).map((x: Int) => x * x)
res2: List[Int] = List(1, 4, 9, 25, 49)
```

Here, (x: Int) => x * x is an anonymous function that takes an argument of type integer and returns its square. Also it is syntactically correct to use infix notation.

```
scala> List(1, 2, 3, 5, 7) map ((x: Int) => x * x)
res2: List[Int] = List(1, 4, 9, 25, 49)
```

Further, parentheses could be replaced by curly braces, as shown below.

```
scala> List(1, 2, 3, 5, 7) map {(x: Int) => x * x}
res2: List[Int] = List(1, 4, 9, 25, 49)
```

Let's say we would like to find the square of all the even numbers below 10. The code snippet below uses *filter*, which takes an anonymous function as a parameter. The first anonymous function takes a number and checks if it is divisible by 2. If a number is divisible by 2, it returns true, otherwise it returns false. Based on this truth value, numbers are filtered, and the result is an array with even numbers.

For the result array, the map method uses a function that takes an integer and multiplies it by itself, which results in the square. This function is applied to every number in the filtered array and hence we get the square of all even numbers below 10. Please note that the pipe sign has nothing to do with the anonymous function; it just means continuation of the code in the Scala interpreter. If you press the *enter* key for incomplete code, you will get it automatically.

```
scala> Array(1,2,3,4,5,6,7,8,9).filter(
| (x:Int) => x % 2 == 0).map((x: Int) => x * x)
res11: Array[Int] = Array(4, 16, 36, 64)
```

9.3 Functions as Values

In Scala, a function can be assigned to a variable and passed around as if it is a value. This makes it convenient to implement algorithms as functions and apply those algorithms to certain data. This is one of the reasons why Scala is a preferred language in the big data area.

```scala
scala> val cubeFun = (x: Int) => x * x * x
cubeFun: Int => Int = <function1>

scala> List(1,2,3,4,5).map(cubeFun)
res12: List[Int] = List(1, 8, 27, 64, 125)
```

In the code snippet, first a function is assigned to an indentifier *cubeFun*. This function calculates the cube of an integer. Next, *map* is invoked on the list and it takes *cubeFun* as a parameter. So the map takes a list and then applies the cube function to each member of the list, and returns the resultant list.

We can also have multiple statements in the function literal as shown below; multiple statements should be enclosed by curly braces. The function returns the value created by evaluating the last statement in the function literal. So if we change the order of statements, we get a different result. This is an important point to remember, as the wrong order of statements creates the wrong results, and it might be time consuming to spot the fix if it is a complex program.

```scala
scala> var square = (x: Int) => {println(x); x * x}
square: Int => Int = <function1>

scala> List(1,2,3,4).map(square)
1
2
3
4
res17: List[Int] = List(1, 4, 9, 16)
```

9.4 Function Parameters

A function can be passed as a parameter to another function. In the code snippet below, *doubleFun* is a function that takes an integer as a parameter and doubles it. Next, the map method takes takes the function *doubleFun* as a parameter and applies it to each number in the sequence; the result is a vector.

```scala
scala> val doubleFun = (x: Int) => 2 * x
doubleFun: Int => Int = <function1>
```

```
scala> (1 to 5).map(doubleFun)
res21: scala.collection.immutable.IndexedSeq[Int] =
  Vector(2, 4, 6, 8, 10)
```

Scala methods can be converted to functions. For example, the following code snippet imports from the package *scala.math*; the underscore immediately after the dot means everything. Then the identifier is assigned a function *ceil*; here, the underscore means function and there should be a space between the word 'ceil' and the underscore. Next, the function *upper* is applied to 1.4, which gives 2.0. Finally, we have *upper* taking *upper* as a parameter with two levels of embedding.

```
scala> import scala.math._
import scala.math._

scala> val upper = ceil _
upper: Double => Double = <function1>

scala> upper(1.4)
res22: Double = 2.0

scala> upper(2.2 + upper(upper(1.2)+ 3.6))
res28: Double = 9.0
```

9.5 Higher Order Functions

When a function is passed to another function as a parameter, the combination becomes a higher order function. We have already seen several such examples in previous sections. Let's discuss a few more interesting examples. The code snippet below has a string containing a list of words, which are split into separate words. *sortWith* takes a binary function that compares two words. The end result is a sorted array.

```
scala> "Lime apple Orange".split(" ")
  .sortWith(_.toLowerCase < _.toLowerCase)
res47: Array[String] = Array(apple, Lime, Orange)
```

Similarly, the following code snippet shows another example of higher order functions. Here we add numbers between 1 and 5, using *reduceRight*, which takes a binary function to perform addition. The whole expression is equivalent to $(1 + (2 + (3 + (4 + 5))))$. If we had used *reduceLeft*, it would have been $((((1 + 2) + 3) + 4) + 5)$.

```
scala> (1 to 5).reduceRight(_ + _)
res48: Int = 15
```

If we analyze both the code snippets, we find something common—the code is concise. Try to write the same program without using functions and higher order functions, and see how long it becomes. Also these code snippets are fairly convenient to analyze. Now this should give us intuition on why Scala is a better language for analytics and big data. Big data involves heavy analytics, in addition to the distributed nature of programming. Functional programming makes it convenient to distribute computational tasks.

9.6 Closures

Scala allows us to use free variables in the definition of a function. In the code snippet below, *product* is a free variable. Since the function literal has a free variable, *(1 to 5).foreach(product += _)* is an open term. An open term requires variable binding during run time, when a function value is created. When binding of free variables happens, it is like closing the function and hence the name *closure*.

```
scala> var product = 1
product: Int = 1

scala> (1 to 5).foreach(product *= _)

scala> product
res62: Int = 120
```

In contrast, the function *area* has a closed term, because *length* and *breadth* are defined within the function definition and the term *length * breadth* has variables, which are always in scope. The variable binding information is available within the function definition and hence such terms are known as closed terms.

```
scala> def area(length: Int, breadth: Int) =
  length * breadth
area: (length: Int, breadth: Int)Int
```

9.7 Currying

Currying is a technique by which a function with one argument list can be converted to a function with multiple argument lists. In the code snippet below, the function *sumOfThreeNums* is an example of non-curried style, which takes all three arguments as a single parameter list and performs the addition. In contrast, the function *curriedSumOfThreeNums* takes one argument list at a time and applies it, which results in a function for the second argument and so on.

```
scala> def sumOfThreeNums(x: Int, y: Int, z: Int) =
```

```
   x + y + z
sumOfThreeNums: (x: Int, y: Int, z: Int)Int

scala> def curriedSumOfThreeNums(x: Int)(y: Int)
  (z: Int) = x + y + z
curriedSumOfThreeNums: (x: Int)(y: Int)(z: Int)Int

scala> sumOfThreeNums(2,3,4)
res65: Int = 9

scala> curriedSumOfThreeNums(2)(3)(4)
res66: Int = 9
```

Let's take one more example. Here we have a curried function that takes three parameter lists for first name, middle name, and last name, respectively. The function then forms a complete name, based on these parameter lists. Please note that we have only one member in each list. A partial name can be formed by supplying partial lists, as shown in the code snippet. The underscore provides a place holder for the third parameter list. So we can use the function *partialName* and supply the remaining list in order to form a full name.

```
scala> def name(fName: String)(mName: String)
  (lName: String) = fName + " " + mName + " " + lName
name: (fName: String)(mName: String)
  (lName: String)String

scala> val partialName = name("Charles")("Anthony")_
partialName: String => String = <function1>

scala> val fullName = partialName("Darwin")
fullName: String = Charles Anthony Darwin
```

The advantage of doing this may not be obvious with this small code snippet. It is allowing us to perform partial computation. If it is in a distributed environment, which has different timing for those three lists, then partial computation helps us to continue with our computational steps, i. e., continue creating the combination of first names and middle names, which is an intermediate result. Whenever the last name cluster is available, we can form the full names, by calling *partialName*.

Of course, this is an oversimplified version of the process. There are Scala based frameworks, dedicated to this kind of distributed computing, for big data. Since functional programming is much closer to mathematics, its reasoning for correctness and soundness is much more convenient compared with imperative programming.

9.8 Writing New Control Structures

Writing new control structures is convenient with higher order functions. Let's define a control structure that invokes a function. In the code snippet below, we define a function *funPrint*, which prints a string, which it receives as a parameter. Please note that the pipe sign that the Scala interpreter automatically inserts in a new line has been removed. Next, we define a function called *invoke*, which invokes a function. Also it accepts a parameter for the function to be called. Finally, we invoke a function, making use of our custom new control structure. This shows how efficient it is to write domain specific language (DSL) using Scala.

```scala
scala> def funPrint = (toPrint: String) =>
  {println(toPrint)}
  funPrint: String => Unit

scala> def invoke(name: String =>
  Unit, param: String) = name(param)
invoke: (name: String => Unit, param: String)Unit

scala> invoke(funPrint,
  "Hello Functional Programming!")
Hello Functional Programming!
```

Next, let's write a double-if control structure that checks two conditions, then executes the code block if both the conditions are true. Figure 9.2 presents a complete solution. If we look at the function definition for *doubleIf*, we see that it takes three arguments; the first two represent test conditions and the third one represents the code to be executed when both the test conditions evaluate to true.

Please note that the function has been defined within the main method; this is an example of a local function. From the main method, we are making a function call by supplying necessary parameters. The first test condition contains two conditions to test. As long as it evaluates to a *Boolean* value, we can have any number of conditions. The second condition has only one condition to check. The third parameter list contains the code block to be executed when both the conditions are satisfied. So the output for this program is:

```
Rank: Exceptional.
Qualified for scholarship.
```

Please note that it is a relatively short program compared with many programs that we wrote earlier in this book. Yet, we were able to define a new control structure. This is one of the areas where functional programming is most productive.

```scala
object DoubleIfApp {
   def main(args: Array[String]): Unit = {
      val age = 21
      val numCollegeDegree = 1
      doubleIf(age > 18 && age < 22)(numCollegeDegree > 0) {
         println("Rank: Exceptional.")
         println("Qualified for scholarship.")
      }

      def doubleIf(test1: => Boolean)(test2: => Boolean)
       (codeBlock: => Unit): Unit = {
         if(test1 && test2){
            codeBlock
         }
      }
   }
}
```

Fig. 9.2: Writing a New Control Structure

9.9 Conclusion

In this chapter, we talked about the history of mathematical functions and how Scala functions are related to mathematical functions. Then we discussed functions as methods. Scala allows us to convert methods into functions. Also we don't have to necessarily name a function. We discussed functions as values to demonstrate functions as first class citizens. Higher order functions are those functions that have functions as parameters. This is one of the powerful features of Scala that enables us to write our own control structures. Next, we covered closures and currying. Finally, we wrote a couple of our own control structures.

9.10 Review Questions

1. When do Scala methods become Scala functions?
2. How can we explicitly convert methods to functions?
3. Identify the anonymous function in the following code snippet.

```scala
scala> Array(1, 2, 3) map ((x: Int) => x + 3)
res0: Array[Int] = Array(4, 5, 6)
```

4. What is the output of the following code snippet?

```scala
scala> def sum(x: Int)(y: Int)(z: Int) = x + y + z
sum1: (x: Int)(y: Int)(z: Int)Int

scala> sum(2)(3)(4)
```

5. What is the output of the following code snippet?

```scala
scala> def sum(x: Int) = (y: Int) => (z: Int) =>
  x + y + z
sum: (x: Int) Int => (Int => Int)

scala> sum(2)(3)(4)
```

6. What is the output of the following code snippet?

```scala
scala> val whatFunction = (x: Int) => x + 1 - 1
whatFunction: Int => Int = <function1>

scala> List(1, 3, 5, 7).map(whatFunction)
```

7. What is the output of the following code snippet?

```scala
scala> def whatFunction(x: Int)(y: Int)(z: Int) =
  x * y * z
whatFunction: (x: Int)(y: Int)(z: Int)Int

scala> val whatFunction1 = whatFunction(2)(3)_
whatFunction1: Int => Int = <function1>

scala> val whatFunction2 = whatFunction1(4)
```

9.11 Problems

1. Write a program to calculate the factorial of a number, using a function.
2. For a given string, write a program to split strings into words and sort them based on their length. Make use of a higher order function to achieve this computational goal.
3. Write a new control structure called *checkedWhile*, which is similar to while except it does not allow a negative loop counting variable.

9.12 Answers to Review Questions

1. Scala methods become Scala functions when we explicitly convert the methods to functions. Also methods in singleton objects are more like functions, as these methods do not associate with multiple instances.
2. We can convert methods to functions by using underscore after the name of the functions. For example, if there is a method called *calculateArea*, *val calArea = calculateArea* _ converts the method to a function and assigns it to the identifier,

calArea. Now, *calArea* can be treated like a function. If the method *calculateArea* takes parameters, *calArea* will take those parameters with the same signature.

3. *(x: Int) => x + 3*
4. 9
5. 9
6. List[Int] = List(1, 3, 5, 7)
7. 24

9.13 Solutions to Problems

1.
```scala
object FactorialApp {
    def main(args: Array[String]): Unit = {
       val num = 5
       println(factorial(num))

       def factorial(number: Integer): Long = {
          if(number == 0)
             return 1
          else
             return number * factorial(number - 1)
       }
    }
}
```

2.
```scala
object WordSortingApp {
    def main(args: Array[String]): Unit = {
       val givenString = "Scala is Fun"
       val sortedWords = givenString.split(" ")
        .sortWith(_.length < _.length)
       sortedWords.foreach(println)
    }
}
```

3.
```
object CheckedWhileApp {
    def main(args: Array[String]): Unit = {
        var i = 1
        checkedWhile(i > 0)(i < 5) {
            println(i)
            i += 1
        }

        def checkedWhile(test1: => Boolean)(test2: => Boolean)
         (codeBlock: => Unit): Unit = {
            while(test1 && test2) {
                codeBlock
            }
        }
    }
}
```

Chapter 10
Pattern Matching

Pattern matching has a long history in computer science and mathematics [Ray65]. Ideas have manifested in different forms. In our day-to-day activities, we perform many pattern matching related thought processes. For example, in order to go to my work place, I need to remember many patterns, including the office building and the road. In fact, as soon as we wake up, our pattern matching starts. How do we know which is the kitchen? We have a pattern stored in our brain, based on previous knowledge activities. These knowledge activities can be reading, talking to somebody and gaining knowledge about kitchens, observing kitchens, etc.

In fact, in order to reach to kitchen, we need to perform other many pattern matching activities. Since these things are done repeatedly, we don't think hard about them. But think about the first time you learned to recognize a kitchen as a kitchen. When did our parents have confidence in us about our mastery? Learning pattern matching is like that. But it will not take as long as it took for us to master different things as children. We already have a significant background knowledge base with us. In this chapter, we will explore how Scala enables us to express pattern matching, in order to achieve our computational goals.

10.1 Case Classes

Case classes can be created by using the modifier *case*, which is a reserved word in Scala, as shown in Table 2.2. These are special classes that can be used in pattern matching. Like regular classes, they can extend from other classes. The parameters are *val* by default. The special thing about a case class is that the compiler automatically generates methods *toString*, *equals*, *hashCode*, and *copy*.

Figure 10.1 shows a typical declaration and use of case classes. Class *Person* is a regular abstract class, which is extended by the case class *Buyer*. We have another case class called *Book*, which has a method called *calculatePrice*. This shows that case classes can have members like regular classes.

© Springer International Publishing AG 2017
B.P. Upadhyaya, *Programming with Scala*, Undergraduate
Topics in Computer Science, https://doi.org/10.1007/978-3-319-69368-2_10

```
abstract class Person(firstName: String, lastName: String)

case class Book(title: String, Author: String,
 priceInUSD: Double) {
    def calculatePrice(quantity: Int): Double = {
       priceInUSD * quantity
    }
}

case class Buyer(fName: String, lName: String,
 location: String)
 extends Person(fName, lName)

object CaseClassApp {
    def main(args: Array[String]): Unit = {
       val book = new Book("Scala","James",4.5)
       val buyer = new Buyer("Charles","Darwin","Palo Alto")
       println(buyer.location)
       println(book.calculatePrice(2))
    }
}
```

Fig. 10.1: Case Classes

10.2 Sealed Classes

Sealed classes provide a mechanism to restrict sub classing a class. A sealed class can only be extended in the same file; any attempt to sub class in a different file is a compile time error. This make it convenient to write a complete pattern matching. If we allow sub classing in a different file or in a different compiler unit, it is hard to track sub classes. If it is hard to track sub classes, then it is hard to write a complete pattern matching. Also, with sealed classes, the Scala compiler is expected to provide a warning message if the pattern matching is not complete.

Figure 10.2 shows a sealed abstract class called *Bird*. The classes *Pigeon*, *Eagle*, and *Duck* inherit from the class *Bird*. The method *whichBird* demonstrates the use of case classes in pattern matching. If the supplied object *bird* matches with type *Pigeon*, then a corresponding message is returned. If none of the other cases match, then the last case takes care of that situation; it is like a fallback.

```
sealed abstract class Bird

case class Pigeon(name: String, owner: String) extends Bird

case class Eagle(name: String, habitat: String) extends Bird

case class Duck(name: String, mode: String) extends Bird

object SealedClassApp {
   def main(args: Array[String]): Unit = {
      println(whichBird(Pigeon("Hem","James")))
   }

   def whichBird(bird: Bird): String = bird match {
      case Pigeon(_,_) => "Detected pigeon."
      case Eagle(_,_) => "Detected eagle."
      case Duck(_,_) => "Detected duck."
      case _ => "No match."
   }
}
```

Fig. 10.2: Sealed Class

10.3 Variable Patterns

A variable pattern enables us to match any object and then process that object further. Figure 10.3 demonstrates a typical variable pattern. For the first matching pattern, we have three cases. The first case matches the incoming string with "Sigma"; if it is a match, it returns "Sigma case". The second case matches the incoming string with "alpha" and then returns "Alpha case", if it is a match. The third case is a bit different, it is more like a default case and matches any object and binds that object with a variable name called *name*. Then it returns a string, which is a concatenation of "Received" and the incoming object. The identifier *matchResult1* is assigned a value returned by the pattern matching.

For the second matching pattern, everything else is the same except the last case, which is known as *wildcard pattern*. This pattern matches any object but doesn't bind it to a name for further processing. We use this pattern, if we do not need to process the object further.

```
object VariablePatternsApp {
    def main(args: Array[String]): Unit = {
        val matchResult1 = "be"+"ta" match {
            case "Sigma" => "Sigma case"
            case "alpha" => "Alpha case"
            case name => "Received " + name
        }
        println(matchResult1)

        val matchResult2 = "be"+"ta" match {
            case "Sigma" => "Sigma case"
            case "alpha" => "Alpha case"
            case _ => "Received something else"
        }
        println(matchResult2)
    }
}
```

Fig. 10.3: Variable Pattern

10.4 Type Patterns

Type patterns or typed patterns enable us to test types. Figure 10.4 presents an example to demonstrate typed patterns. When 2.5 is passed to the function *detectType*, it matches with type *Double*. So the function returns string "Double", which is then printed on the console. Similarly, when the string "Test" is passed to the function *detectType*, the type matches with *String*. Accordingly, "String" is returned to the caller and eventually printed on the console.

```
object TypedPatternsApp {
    def main(args: Array[String]): Unit = {
        println(detectType(2.5))
        println(detectType("Test"))

        def detectType(len: Any): String = len match {
            case x: Int => "Integer"
            case y: Double => "Double"
            case z: String => "String"
            case _ => "Unknown type"
        }
    }
}
```

Fig. 10.4: Type Pattern

Now, what happens if we supply 2.5*f* to the function *detectType*. Even though double precision numbers are similar to floating point numbers, the types are not the same. Since we have specifically mentioned that the type is *Float*, there should be a case to catch *Float* type. Since there is no such case, it falls to default. The default case returns "Unknown type", which is then printed on the console.

10.5 Literal Patterns

We can use literals in pattern matching, as shown in Figure 10.5. The first case matches the input with the literal "Scala". If it is a match, the string literal "Scala" is returned back to the caller. In this case, the caller prints it on the console. The second case matches the input with the *Boolean* literal *false*; if it is a match, the literal "false" is returned. Similarly the literal "five" is returned, if the input is integer value 5.

```
object LiteralPatternsApp {
    def main(args: Array[String]): Unit = {
        println(detectLiterals("Scala"))
        println(detectLiterals(6.7f))
        println(detectLiterals(Nil))

        def detectLiterals(input: Any) = input match {
            case "Scala" => "Scala"
            case false => "false"
            case 5 => "five"
            case 6.7f => "Six decimal seven float"
            case _ => "Unknown case"
        }
    }
}
```

Fig. 10.5: Literal Pattern

For floating point, it should be exactly 6.7*f*, because if we supply 6.7 then we are supplying 6.7 of type *Double*, which is not the same as 6.7 of type *Float*. For an exact match, "Six decimal seven float" is returned to the caller. Finally, the last case is the default case, i.e., if the input does not match with any other cases, it matches with the default case, returning "Unknown case" to the caller. So, the output of this program is as shown below.

```
Scala
Six decimal seven float
Unknown case
```

10.6 Constructor Patterns

Constructor patterns provide some of the most powerful pattern matching abilities in Scala. Also these patterns allows us to match to any level of depth, called deep matching. Figure 10.6 shows a typical implementation of constructor patterns. We have three case classes. The case class *Number* takes one integer type of argument and constructs a *Number*. Similarly, *RealNumber* takes numerator and denominator to create a real number. The last case class, *ComplexNumber*, takes takes two real numbers and creates a complex number.

```scala
case class Number(num: Int)

case class RealNumber(num: Number, den: Number)

case class ComplexNumber(reaPart: RealNumber,
 imgPart:RealNumber) {
   def complexNumber() = {
      val imgNumber = reaPart + " + i * " + imgPart
      imgNumber
   }
}

object ConstructorPatternsApp {
   def main(args: Array[String]): Unit = {
      construct(Number(0))
      construct(ComplexNumber(RealNumber(Number(2), Number(7)),
       RealNumber(Number(8), Number(9))))
      construct(Some("apple", 1, 2.5))

      def construct(x: Any) = x match {
         case Number(0) => println("Integer value zero")
         case RealNumber(Number(2), Number(5)) =>
          println("Real number 2/5")
         case ComplexNumber(RealNumber(Number(2), Number(7)),
          RealNumber(Number(8), Number(9))) =>
          println(y.imaginaryNumber)
         case _ => println("No match")
      }
   }
}
```

Fig. 10.6: Constructor Pattern

The *construct* function takes an argument of type *Any* and tries to match with one of the four cases. The first case matches input with type *Number* as well as the value 0. So it already does two levels of matching. The second case does three levels of matching. The first level is the type *RealNumber*, the second level is the type *Number*, and the third level is a value match. Similarly, the third case does four levels of matching—type *ComplexNumber*, type *RealNumber*, type *Number*, and values. If a match occurs, it invokes the method *complexNumber* on object *y*, which is the name assigned for the complex number created in that case. Finally, the last case is the default case, i. e., if no other cases match, then the input matches with this wild card case and returns the string "No match". So, the output of this program is as shown below. Line number 2 and line number 3 are printed on the same line. We split it here to fit the width of the book.

```
Integer value zero
RealNumber(Number(2),Number(7))  +
 i * RealNumber(Number(8),Number(9))
No match
```

10.7 Tuple Patterns

A tuple pattern matches an input with a tuple; this pattern does not match the values. Figure 10.7 demonstrates a typical tuple pattern implementation. The function *detectTuple* has four cases. The first case matches the input *x* with a tuple with two elements. If the input is a tuple with two elements, then this is the match and those two elements are printed on the console. Similarly, the second case matches the input with a tuple containing three elements. If there is a match, all the elements are printed.

```
object TuplePatternsApp {
    def main(args: Array[String]): Unit = {
        detectTuple(1)
        detectTuple(2,4)
        detectTuple(1,"test",5,7)

        def detectTuple(x: Any) = x match {
            case (a, b) => println(a + "," + b)
            case (a,b,c) => println(a + "," + b + "," + c)
            case (a,b,c,d) => println(a+","+b+","+c+","+d)
            case _ => println("No match")
        }
    }
}
```

Fig. 10.7: Tuple Pattern

The third case matches the input with a tuple containing four elements. All four elements are printed, if it is a match. Finally, the default case provides the fall back. If the input does not match with any other cases, then it is matched with the default case, because it has a wild card matching pattern. For the default case, the output is "No match". The output of this program is:

```
No match
2,4
1,test,5,7
```

10.8 Extractor Patterns

An extractor pattern, as the name suggests, helps us to extract different parts. Figure 10.8 shows a typical implementation of an extractor patter for United States (US) phone numbers. US phone numbers are 11-digit numbers with different separators. One of the common separators is hyphen (-).

```scala
object Phone {
    def apply(countryCode: Int, areaCode: Int,
      part1: Int, part2: Int) = {
        countryCode+"-"+areaCode+"-"+part1+"-"+part2
    }
    def unapply(phoneNumber: String): Option[(String, String,
      String, String)] = {
        val parts = phoneNumber.split("-")
        if(parts.length == 4) {
            Some(parts(0), parts(1), parts(2), parts(3))
        } else {
            None
        }
    }
}

object ExtractorPatternsApp {
    def main(args: Array[String]): Unit = {
        extractPhone("1-650-324-5674")
        extractPhone("1-304-506")

        def extractPhone(x: Any) = x match {
            case Phone(country,area,pt1,pt2) =>
            println("country code: "+country+", "+"area code: "+
            area+", "+"part1: "+pt1+", "+"part2: "+pt2)
            case _ => println("No match")
        }
    }
}
```

Fig. 10.8: Extractor Pattern

In the program, we see a singleton object called *Phone*, which has *apply* and *unapply* methods. These are standard methods that the compiler recognizes, in order to construct and de-construct the object, *Phone* in this case. The *apply* method takes four different parts and then constructs a phone number. As opposed to that, the *unapply* methods takes a string, which is a complete phone number, and splits it into meaningful parts, as shown in the program.

From the main method, we are making two calls: one with a proper number and the other with incomplete parts. For the first call, it matches with the extractor pattern and then prints all the parts—*country code, area code, part1*, and *part2*. Since the second call does not have a proper number, it falls to the default case and the corresponding message is printed. The output for this program is (divided to fit the width of the book):

```
country code: 1, area code: 650,
 part1: 324, part2: 5674
No match
```

10.9 Sequence Patterns

Sequence patterns enable us to match sequences. Figure 10.9 demonstrates *List* and *Array* pattern matching. The *detectSequence* method takes the input and tries to match it with one of the cases. The first case matches the input with an array containing three elements; the first two elements should be 0 and 0, the third element can be anything. The second case matches a list containing two elements; the first element should be 1 and second element can be anything. The third case matches with a variable length list. In order to match, the list should have at least one element and its value must be 0. After that, the list can have any number of elements, with any type. The variables *a* and *b* bind the matching object so that the object can be processed further. The final case is the default case.

```
object SequencePaternsApp {
    def main(args: Array[String]): Unit = {
        detectSequence(Array(0,0,"test"))
        detectSequence(Array(0,1,2))
        detectSequence(List(1,3))
        detectSequence(List("delta","sigma"))
        detectSequence(List(0,"test",3))

        def detectSequence(x: Any) = x match {
            case a @ Array(0,0,_) => println(a(0),a(1),a(2))
            case b @ List(1,_) => println(b(0),b(1))
            case List(0,_*) =>
             println("Matched with variable length list")
            case _ => println("No match")
        }
    }
}
```

Fig. 10.9: Sequence Pattern

Now, let's analyze each call. The first call has a parameter, which is an array containing three elements. The first two are 0 and 0 respectively, and the last one is a string. In the first match clause, we have the first two elements as 0 and 0 respectively, and the last element is anything. So it matches with the first case, printing all three elements of the array on the console. In the second call, the first and the third elements match but the second element does not and hence it matches with the default case.

The third call matches with the second case and outputs two elements on the console. The fourth call has two parameters, which are strings. There is no case that has a list with the first element as a string, and hence it falls to the default case. The fifth call has the first element matching with the third case. The third case matches with a variable length list, which has only the first element fixed. The remaining elements could be of any type and there can be any number of elements. At the minimum, in order to match, the input should have at least one element; the value must be 0, if it is the first element. So, the output of this program is:

```
(0,0,test)
No match
(1,3)
No match
Matched with variable length list
```

10.10 XML Patterns

XML patterns can be used to process XML data. Figure 10.10 demonstrates a typical application of XML patterns. The function *detectXML* takes *scala.xml.Node* type of object and tries to match it with one of the cases. Please note that you need to include something equivalent to *libraryDependencies += "org.scala-lang" % "scala-xml" % "2.11.0-M4"*, in your *build.sbt* file, if you are using an SBT project to program and using Scala version 2.11.0 or higher. The version can be different than shown here, based on your other setup parameters. This dependency fetches the necessary jar file so that we can use XML library.

The first case matches data for a first name; the XML representation is *<firstName ></firstName >*. Similarly, the second case matches a last name. If incoming data does not match either of these cases, then it falls into the default case, which prints "No match" on the console. We will discuss XML processing details in Chapter 14. The output for the program in Figure 10.10 is as shown below.

```
First name: Charles
Last name: Darwin
No match
```

```
object XMLPatternsApp {
    def main(args: Array[String]): Unit = {
        detectXML(<firstName>Charles</firstName>)
        detectXML(<lastName>Darwin</lastName>)
        detectXML(<Phone>111-222-4567</Phone>)

        def detectXML(x: scala.xml.Node) = x match {
            case <firstName>{content}</firstName> =>
              println("First name: "+content)
            case <lastName>{content}</lastName> =>
              println("Last name: "+content)
            case _ => println("No match")
        }
    }
}
```

Fig. 10.10: XML Pattern

10.11 Conclusion

In this chapter, we first discussed case classes, which can be used in pattern matching. Then we covered sealed classes. Once a class is sealed, it can only be extended
in the same file, thereby making it convenient for developers to write complete
match cases. We then covered numerous patterns. Variable patterns enable us to
bind a matched object with a name so that object can be processed further. A wildcard pattern uses underscore (_) to represent any. Generally, it is used for a default
case. A type pattern enables us to perform type checking. Literal patterns, as the
name suggests, are to match with literals. Constructor patterns help us to check the
construction process. This is one of the most powerful pattern matching features in
Scala. A tuple pattern enables us to match with tuples and to process tuple elements
further. Extractor patterns are used to extract parts of a whole. Sequence patterns
enable us to match with sequences, like *Array*, *List*, etc. Finally, we discussed XML
patterns, which allow us to match and to process XML data.

10.12 Review Questions

1. Write one application of case classes.
2. Why do we need to seal a class?
3. What is the benefit of variable in a variable pattern?
4. Which pattern is the best candidate for type matching?
5. What is the name of pattern that helps us to match literals?
6. Theoretically, is there a limit for the depth level in constructor matching?
7. If a function called *tupMatch(x: Any)* contains a case: *case (a,b,c) =>*, what is
   the output for *tupMatch(2,3,4)*?

8. If a function called *seqMatch(x: Any)* contains a case: *case a @ List(0, _*) =>*
   println(a(0)), what is the output for *seqMatch(List(0,1,2))*?
9. For the function mentioned in the previous problem, is the output always 0?
10. If a function called *detXML(x: scala.xml.Node)* has a case: *<phone >{content}*
    </phone > =>, how can we extract phone data?

10.13 Problems

1. Using pattern matching, write a program to detect the type of given data. You can
   restrict to your types to *Int*, *Double*, *Char*, and *String*.
2. There are two fruits baskets—A and B. Basket A contains an even number of
   apples and an odd number of oranges; basket B contains an odd number of apples
   and an even number of oranges. For a given number of apples and oranges, write
   a program to detect which basket the combinations were picked from. Here are
   the rules:

   a. If an odd number of apples and an even number of oranges are required, these
      should be picked from basket B.
   b. If an even number of apples and an odd number of oranges are required, these
      should be picked from basket A.
   c. If an even number of apples and an even number of oranges are required, these
      should be picked from somewhere else.

3. Using pattern matching, find whether a given array contains an odd number of
   elements or an even number of elements. For both the cases, find how many
   elements are odd numbers and how many are even numbers.

10.14 Answers to Review Questions

1. Case classes can be used for pattern matching.
2. We seal a class so that it cannot be sub classed from files other than where it is
   located. This makes it convenient for developers to write complete match cases.
3. A variable in a variable pattern allows us to process the matched object further.
4. A type pattern is the best candidate for type matching.
5. Literal pattern
6. Theoretically, there is no limit for the depth level in constructor matching.
7. It is a match; but the right side of the lambda expression does not have anything,
   so it does not do anything.
8. 0
9. Yes, the output is always 0. In order for a match to occur, the first element of the
   input list should always be 0. The right side of the lambda expression prints the
   first element of the matched input list.

10. The identifier *content* binds the matching phone data, use *content* for extraction.

10.15 Solutions to Problems

1.
```scala
object TypeDetectionApp {
    def main(args: Array[String]): Unit = {
      val givenData = "Functional programming"
      detectType(givenData)

      def detectType(x: Any) = x match {
        case x: Int => println(x + " is of Int type.")
        case x: Double => println(x + " is of Double type.")
        case x: Char => println(x + " is of Char type.")
        case x: String => println(x + " is of String type.")
        case _ => println("Some other type.")
      }
    }
}
```

2.
```scala
object CombDetectionApp {
    def main(args: Array[String]): Unit = {
      detectBasket(List("apples",3,"oranges",3))

      def detectBasket(x: Any) = x match {
        case List(a,b,c,d) if(b.asInstanceOf[Int] % 2 == 0 &&
        d.asInstanceOf[Int] % 2 != 0) =>
        println("Picked from basket A")
        case List(a,b,c,d) if(b.asInstanceOf[Int] % 2 != 0 &&
        d.asInstanceOf[Int] % 2 == 0) =>
        println("Picked from basket B")
        case _ => println("Picked from somewhere else.")
      }
    }
}
```

```scala
3. object EvenAndOddNumApp {
    def main(args: Array[String]): Unit = {
      detectEvenOrOdd(Array(2,2,5,2,1))

      def detectEvenOrOdd(x: Array[Int]) = x match {
        case a @ Array(_*) if(a.size % 2 == 0) => {
          println("Even number of elements.")
          detectElements(a)
        }
        case b @ Array(_*) if(b.size % 2 != 0) => {
          println("Odd number of elements.")
          detectElements(b)
        }
        case _ => println("Something went wrong.")
      }

      def detectElements(x: Array[Int]): Unit = {
        var oddCount = 0
        var evenCount = 0
        for (elem <- x) {
          if (elem % 2  == 0) {
            evenCount += 1
          } else if(elem % 2 != 0) {
            oddCount += 1
          } else {
            println("Wrong element.")
          }
        }
        println("Total number of even elements: "+evenCount)
        println("Total number of odd elements: "+oddCount)
      }
    }
}
```

Chapter 11
List Processing

In our day-to-day lives, we need to deal with lists in a regular basis. For example, if we are going to buy groceries, we make a grocery list. Also we tend to list items for mental clarity, when we are planning. If we are moving from one place to another and would like to delegate the task to a mover, then we make lists of items. Also, movers make their own list of items accepted for moving and use that list as an important element of the moving contract. So lists are everywhere.

Scala brings together features from different programming paradigms. With one set of syntactical elements, we can program in multiple paradigms. In this chapter, we discuss Scala's features that enable us to model real world list processing.

11.1 List Construction

Lists can be constructed using Scala's collection library. Each element of the list is separated by a comma and strings should be inside double quotes, as usual. The list, *cityList*, in the following code snippet, contains three elements of type *String*. The index starts from 0, so the first city can be accessed using *cityList(0)*. The size of the list can be found by executing *citiList.size*, as shown in the code snippet.

```
scala> val cityList = List("Sunnyvale", "San Jose",
 "Palo Alto")
cityList: List[String] = List(Sunnyvale, San Jose,
 Palo Alto)

scala> cityList.size
res0: Int = 3
```

Scala lists can contain elements of different types. If elements are of different types then the type of the list is *Any*. The way to access list element does not change even if the list contains elements of different types. But the type of element is converted to a common type *Any*. So if we need to treat an element as a specific type,

© Springer International Publishing AG 2017
B.P. Upadhyaya, *Programming with Scala*, Undergraduate
Topics in Computer Science, https://doi.org/10.1007/978-3-319-69368-2_11

we need to first type cast. Also the type specific operations are available after a successful type cast.

```scala
scala> val bag = List("book", 2, "pen")
bag: List[Any] = List(book, 2, pen)

scala> bag(0)
res2: Any = book
```

The list construction process is right associative, as shown in the code snippet below. If we remove the parentheses, the Scala interpreter will still construct a list from right to left, i. e., starting with an empty list, *Nil*. The two consecutive colons (::), pronounced *cons*, is a list extension operator and a new element is added in the front of the list. If there is no element in the list to be concatenated, the new element is concatenated with an empty list, *Nil*.

```scala
scala> val cityList = "Sunnyvale" :: ("San Jose" ::
  ("Palo Alto" :: Nil))
cityList: List[String] = List(Sunnyvale, San Jose,
  Palo Alto)
```

11.2 Operations

Lists support various interesting operations. There are three fundamental operations, which form the basis for remaining operations. *head* returns the first element of the list and *tail* returns all elements of the list except the first; *isEmpty* returns true if the list is empty, otherwise it returns false.

```scala
scala> cityList.head
res6: String = Sunnyvale

scala> cityList.tail
res7: List[String] = List(San Jose, Palo Alto)

scala> cityList.isEmpty
res8: Boolean = false
```

Let's define a list called *lett* as *val lett = List("a", "b", "c")*; we will use this list to demonstrate various operations.

1. *head* : It returns the first element of the list. Example: *lett.head* returns a.
2. *tail* : It returns all the elements except the first one. Example. *lett.tail* returns *List(b, c)*.
3. *isEmpty* : It returns a *Boolean value*. If the list is empty, it returns *true*, otherwise it returns *false*. Example: *lett.isEmpty* returns false.

4. *Nil* : It means empty list. Example:

```
scala> val a = Nil
a: scala.collection.immutable.Nil.type = List()

scala> a.size
res16: Int = 0
```

5. *List()* : It is equivalent to *Nil*.
6. *last* : It gives the last element of the list. Example:

```
scala> lett.last
res17: String = c
```

7. *::* : It is a list extension operator; the newest element is added in the front of the list. Example:

```
scala> "z" :: lett
res18: List[String] = List(z, a, b, c)
```

8. *:::* : It concatenates two lists. Example:

```
scala> val num = List(1,2,3)
num: List[Int] = List(1, 2, 3)

scala> num ::: lett
res21: List[Any] = List(1, 2, 3, a, b, c)
```

9. *<ListName >(<index >)* : It provides a way to access a list element; list index starts from 0. Example:

```
scala> lett(0)
res22: String = a
```

10. *count* : It returns the count of elements satisfying certain criteria. Example:

```
scala> lett.count(x => x < "c")
res26: Int = 2
```

11. *drop* : It drops the specified number of elements from the beginning of the list. Example:

```
scala> lett.drop(1)
res29: List[String] = List(b, c)
```

12. *dropRight* : It drops the specified number of elements from the end of the list. Example:

```
scala> lett.dropRight(1)
res31: List[String] = List(a, b)
```

13. *exists* : It checks the existence of elements that satisfy certain conditions. Example:

```
scala> lett.exists(x => x == "c")
res32: Boolean = true
```

14. *filter* : It filters the elements based on provided criteria. Example:

```
scala> lett.filter(x => x < "c")
res33: List[String] = List(a, b)
```

15. *forall* : It applies given criteria to all elements of the list. Example:

```
scala> lett.forall(x => x < "z")
res36: Boolean = true
```

16. *foreach* : It applies given criteria or functions to each element of the list. Example:

```
scala> lett.foreach(x => print(x))
abc
```

17. *init* : It returns a list containing all the elements except the last element. Example:

```
scala> lett.init
res38: List[String] = List(a, b)
```

18. *length* : It returns the size of the list. Example:

```
scala> lett.length
res40: Int = 3
```

19. *map* : It returns a list, which is the result of applying a function passed as a parameter. Example:

```
scala> lett.map(x => x + "e")
res41: List[String] = List(ae, be, ce)
```

20. *mkstring* : It converts all the elements of the list to a single string. Example:

```
scala> lett.mkString
res44: String = abc

scala> lett.mkString("-")
res45: String = a-b-c
```

21. *reverse* : It reverses the order of elements in the list and returns the newly ordered list. Example:

```
scala> lett.reverse
res52: List[String] = List(c, b, a)
```

22. *sorted* : It returns the sorted version of the given list. Example:

```
scala> val nums = List(5,4,7,6)
nums: List[Int] = List(5, 4, 7, 6)

scala> nums.sorted
res61: List[Int] = List(4, 5, 6, 7)
```

11.3 Patterns

In addition to the patterns that we discussed in Chapter 10, lists support additional pattern matching features. These features provide higher flexibility to developers so that they can program for diverse requirements. The members of one list can be transferred to another list by creating a list variable that contains an equal number of elements to that of the source list. Each variable in the target list is bound to the value with the same index in the source list.

```
scala> val drinks = List("Coke","Pepsi","Fanta",
  "Wine")
drinks: List[String] = List(Coke, Pepsi, Fanta, Wine)

scala> val List(p,q,r,s) = drinks
p: String = Coke
q: String = Pepsi
r: String = Fanta
s: String = Wine
```

If we do not know the size of the source list, we can use the *cons* operator as shown below. In this case, we are telling the interpreter that we know there are at least two elements but we don't know how many there are after that. Scala binds the first two elements to the variables that we provided and creates a list for the remaining elements in the source list.

```
scala> val x :: y :: remaining = drinks
x: String = Coke
y: String = Pepsi
remaining: List[String] = List(Fanta, Wine)
```

Now, let's look at a complete program that uses pattern matching to extract the head and tail of a list. Figure 11.1 shows a typical way to extract the head and tail using the *cons* operator. The identifier before the *cons* operator represents the head of the list and the identifier after the *cons* operator represents the tail of the list. The output of this program is:

```
Head: tiger
Size of tail: 2
```

```
object ListExtractionApp {
    def main(args: Array[String]): Unit = {
        extractFromList(List("tiger", "lion", "leopard"))

        def extractFromList(x: List[String]) = x match {
            case a :: b => {
                println("Head: " + a)
                println("Size of tail: " + b.size)
            }
            case _ => println("Malformed input")
        }
    }
}
```

Fig. 11.1: List Extraction

11.4 List Class

The list class has many first order and higher order methods available to facilitate developers with their work. In this section, we discuss some of those, especially the ones that we have not covered so far.

1. *List concatenation (:::)* : The concatenation operator joins two lists and it is right-associative. In the following code snippet, the first list consists of the first three prime numbers and the second list has the next two primes. When these two lists are concatenated, we get the combination as one list. The assigned identifier is res67, so if we execute *res67(4)*, we get the value 7.

```
scala> List(1,2,3) ::: List(5,7)
res67: List[Int] = List(1, 2, 3, 5, 7)
```

2. *take* : It returns a new list with the number of elements mentioned in the parameter; the elements are taken from the beginning of the list. In the code snippet below, *take(3)* returns a list containing the first three primes.

```
scala> List(1,2,3,5).take(3)
res70: List[Int] = List(1, 2, 3)
```

3. *splitAt* : It splits a list into two separate lists at a given index. The split index is included in the second list. In the code snippet below, element 5 is at index 3 and hence is the first element of the second list, after the split.

```
scala> List(1,2,3,5,7).splitAt(3)
res71: (List[Int], List[Int]) = (List(1, 2, 3),
    List(5, 7))
```

4. *zip* : It takes two lists and combines elements having the same index in such a way that they form a pair. So the resultant list is a list of pairs. In the code snippet below, the first list contains indices and the second list contains items. When we zip, we get pairs of indices and items.

```
scala> List(0,1,2) zip List("coke","fanta","pepsi")
res1: List[(Int, String)] = List((0,coke),
  (1,fanta), (2,pepsi))
```

5. *unzip* : It is the reverse process of the zip operation. In the code snippet below, we are re-using the list that we constructed for the previous step. When we unzip the zipped list, we get our original two lists back.

```
scala> res1.unzip
res2: (List[Int], List[String]) = (List(0, 1, 2),
  List(coke, fanta, pepsi))
```

6. *toArray* : It converts a list to an array. Array is a fundamental data structure and is available in most high level programming languages, in one form or another. Scala arrays can contain data of different types; this is achieved by converting elements to a common higher type.

```
scala> List(1,2,3,5).toArray
res3: Array[Int] = Array(1, 2, 3, 5)
```

7. *copyToArray* : It copies the elements of a list to an array. If the index is not specified, elements will be copied from the beginning index, otherwise elements will be copied from the specified index. This is another very useful operation as it allows us to control the data population.

```
scala> val target = new Array[Int](5)
target: Array[Int] = Array(0, 0, 0, 0, 0)

scala> val source = List(3,5)
source: List[Int] = List(3, 5)

scala> source.copyToArray(target,2)

scala> target
res11: Array[Int] = Array(0, 0, 3, 5, 0)
```

8. *map* : It applies a parameterized function to specified elements of a list. In the code snippet below, _ * 2 is a function that takes each element of the list and multiplies it by two. When all the elements are processed, it forms a result, which is a new list with elements doubled. We have covered this method earlier in this book; this is a refresher. We have intentionally repeated many things as it helps us to remember them.

```
scala> List(1,2,3) map (_ * 2)
res14: List[Int] = List(2, 4, 6)
```

9. *flatMap* : Like *map*, it applies a parameterized function to specified elements of a list, but merges the inner lists, as shown below.

```
scala> val oddNumList = List(1,3,5)
oddNumList: List[Int] = List(1, 3, 5)

scala> val evenNumList = List(2,4)
evenNumList: List[Int] = List(2, 4)

scala> val numList = List(oddNumList,evenNumList)
numList: List[List[Int]] = List(List(1, 3, 5),
  List(2, 4))

scala> numList flatMap(_.toList)
res15: List[Int] = List(1, 3, 5, 2, 4)
```

10. *filter*: It filters the elements of a list based on a parameterized predicate. The new
    list contains the elements that satisfy the condition in the predicate. In the code
    snippet below, odd numbers form the new list.

```
scala> List(1,2,3,4) filter (_ % 2 != 0)
res21: List[Int] = List(1, 3)
```

11. *partition* : It partitions a list into two lists, based on criteria expressed in the
    parameterized predicate. Those elements that satisfy the criteria form the first
    list and remaining elements form the second list.

```
scala> List(1,2,3,4) partition (_ % 2 != 0)
res22: (List[Int], List[Int]) = (List(1, 3),
  List(2, 4))
```

12. *find* : It returns the first element that matches the criteria expressed in the param-
    eterized predicate.

```
scala> List(1,2,3,4) find (_ % 2 != 0)
res23: Option[Int] = Some(1)
```

13. *forall* : It returns true if the parameterized predicate holds true for all the elements
    of a list.

```
scala> List(1,3,5,5,7,3) forall (_ % 2 != 0)
res36: Boolean = true
```

14. *exists* : It returns true if the parameterized predicate holds true for at least one
    elements of a list.

```
scala> List(1,3,2,5,5,7,3) exists (_ % 2 == 0)
res39: Boolean = true
```

11.5 List Object

Scala's *List* class has a companion object called *List*, which contains numerous utilities. We discuss some of those utilities here.

1. *List.range* : It creates a *List* for a specified range of elements. The first parameter provides the *from* value and the second parameter provides the *until* value. Also an additional step parameter can be supplied, which can be positive as well as negative.

```scala
scala> List.range(1,7)
res41: List[Int] = List(1, 2, 3, 4, 5, 6)

scala> List.range(1,7,2)
res42: List[Int] = List(1, 3, 5)

scala> List.range(7,1,-2)
res43: List[Int] = List(7, 5, 3)
```

2. *List.fill* : It creates a list by replicating a value. The first parameter provides the dimension or the repeat and the second parameter provides the value; the method takes one parameter at a time. There are several variations of this method.

```scala
scala> List.fill(5)("cat")
res55: List[String] = List(cat, cat, cat, cat, cat)

scala> List.fill(2,3)(1)
res61: List[List[Int]] = List(List(1, 1, 1),
  List(1, 1, 1))
```

3. *List.tabulate* : It creates a list containing values of a specified function, which is the second parameter, over a range of integer values starting from 0. There are several variations of this method.

```scala
scala> List.tabulate(3)(x => x + 1)
res70: List[Int] = List(1, 2, 3)
```

11.6 Conclusion

In this chapter, we started with the list construction process. Then we discussed simple list operations. These operations are handy for analytical programming. We covered list patterns and list element extraction. Next, we discussed additional methods in the *List* class, covering both first order and higher order methods. There are several popular big data processing frameworks, including Apache Spark, that heavily utilize higher order list methods. We also covered some of the utility methods available in the companion object *List*.

11.7 Review Questions

1. Search on the Internet for the word "Lisp" and locate resources for the Lisp programming language. Is there any relationship between Lisp and Scala lists?
2. What is the output of the following code snippet?

```
val mix = List("tomato",2,"pepsi")
```

3. What is the output for *mix.head*?
4. What is the output for *mix.tail*?
5. What is the output for the following code snippet?

```
scala> val oddDigits = List(1,3,5,7,9)
oddDigits: List[Int] = List(1, 3, 5, 7, 9)

scala> val evenDigits = List(2,4,6,8)
evenDigits: List[Int] = List(2, 4, 6, 8)

scala> oddDigits zip evenDigits
```

6. What is the output for the following code snippet?

```
scala> oddDigits exists (x => x%2 == 0)
```

7. What is the output for the following code snippet?

```
scala> oddDigits forall (x => x%2 != 0)
```

8. What is the output for the following code snippet?

```
scala> evenDigits partition (x => x < 6)
```

9. What is the output for the following code snippet?

```
scala> evenDigits take(3)
```

10. What is the output for the following code snippet?

```
scala> oddDigits splitAt(3)
```

11.8 Problems

1. Assume that Basket A contains all apples and Basket B contains all oranges. The number of apples in Basket A is equal to the number of oranges in Basket B. Further, all apples and oranges are numbered starting from 1, in an increasing order, without repeating. Using list, write a program to extract the last apple and orange pair.

2. In the context of the previous problem, add Basket C, which combines the contents of Basket A and Basket B. The criteria for combination is that apples and oranges should be separable without losing the labels. Print the total number of pairs available in Basket C, on the console. Sell the last two pairs and stop the day's transaction.
3. In the context of the previous problem, for the remaining pairs, separate apples from oranges and move them back to their respective baskets. Print the total number of apples and oranges available in each basket, on the console.

11.9 Answers to Review Questions

1. Lisp is the first artificial intelligence high level programming language based on lambda calculus. It is also the second oldest high level programming language, the first being Fortran. Lisp has strong support for list processing. Scala brings together many features, including list processing.
2. mix: List[Any] = List(tomato, 2, pepsi)
3. res71: Any = tomato *(Note: res71 is specific to a particular session, it is ok to have different values)*
4. res72: List[Any] = List(2, pepsi)
5. List[(Int, Int)] = List((1,2), (3,4), (5,6), (7,8))
6. res76: Boolean = false
7. res78: Boolean = true
8. res79: (List[Int], List[Int]) = (List(2, 4),List(6, 8))
9. res80: List[Int] = List(2, 4, 6)
10. res81: (List[Int], List[Int]) = (List(1, 3, 5),List(7, 9))

11.10 Solutions to Problems

1.
```scala
object AppleOrangeBasketApp1 {
    def main(args: Array[String]): Unit = {
        val basketA = List("apple1","apple2","apple3","apple4")
        val basketB =
         List("orange1","orange2","orange3","orange4")
        extractLastPair(basketA, basketB)

        def extractLastPair(apples: List[String],
         oranges: List[String]): Unit = {
           val mix = apples zip oranges
           println(mix(mix.size - 1))
        }
    }
}
```

2.
```scala
object AppleOrangeBasketApp2 {
  def main(args: Array[String]): Unit = {
    val basketA =
     List("apple1", "apple2", "apple3", "apple4")
    val basketB =
     List("orange1", "orange2", "orange3", "orange4")
    val basketC = (basketA zip basketB).dropRight(2)
    basketC.foreach(println)
  }
}
```

3.
```scala
object AppleOrangeBasketApp3 {
  def main(args: Array[String]): Unit = {
    var basketA =
     List("apple1", "apple2", "apple3", "apple4")
    var basketB =
     List("orange1", "orange2", "orange3", "orange4")
    val basketC = (basketA zip basketB).dropRight(2)
    val tempBasket = basketC.unzip
    basketA = tempBasket._1
    basketB = tempBasket._2
    println("Total apples in Basket A: "+basketA.size)
    println("Total oranges in Basket B: "+basketB.size)
  }
}
```

Chapter 12
The Scala Collections Framework

As indicated in Chapter 1, high level programming languages are close to natural languages whenever possible. The Scala collections represent higher level natural language constructs. In some cases, these constructs might represent some mathematical structures for preciseness. We deal with sets of things in our daily lives. Also we need to map some items with some other items. Sometimes, we create indices for faster searching and so on. In this chapter, we discuss sets, maps, different types of sequences, and tuples. All of these collections are frequently used to solve programming problems.

12.1 Mutable versus Immutable Collections

Scala provides two sets of collections—immutable and mutable. Immutable collections are like *val*, i.e., we cannot change them but we can make copies of them. Mutable collections are changeable. While programming, one might suit better than the other depending upon the problem to be solved. But in general, immutable collections are recommended over mutable collections for several reasons.

First of all, immutable collections are modification safe, i. e., if we have a complex distributed environment, then it might be error prone to keep track of who is modifying what. Also it is relatively much more complex to reason about the program because of uncertainties in a distributed environment. In such scenarios, immutable collections can help.

Second of all, immutable collections have relatively compact representations for small collections. This maps to efficiency and performance. So it is good practice to start with immutable collections and move to mutable collections, if required. The other direction can also be adopted but it might be a bit complex to replace all the networked modifications correctly.

© Springer International Publishing AG 2017
B.P. Upadhyaya, *Programming with Scala*, Undergraduate
Topics in Computer Science, https://doi.org/10.1007/978-3-319-69368-2_12

12.2 Sets

A set contains a list of non-repeated elements. So it is obvious when to use set; storing elements in a set guarantees uniqueness. In the code snippet below, a set is created with three elements in it. By default, *Set* from the *scala.collection.immutable* package is used, i.e., we create an immutable collection by default. If we want to change it to mutable, then we can import the *scala.collection.mutable* package and then the corresponding collection.

```scala
scala> val cities =
  Set("Sunnyvale", "San Jose", "Palo Alto")
cities: scala.collection.immutable.Set[String] =
  Set(Sunnyvale, San Jose, Palo Alto)
```

Sets support numerous operations.

1. **+** : It adds an element to a set. In the following code snippet, the first fragment creates a set containing numbers from 1 to 5. The second fragment adds number 6 to the *numSet*.

```scala
scala> val numSet = Set(1,2,3,4,5)
numSet: scala.collection.immutable.Set[Int] =
  Set(5, 1, 2, 3, 4)

scala> numSet + 6
res11: scala.collection.immutable.Set[Int] =
  Set(5, 1, 6, 2, 3, 4)
```

2. **-** : It removes an element from a set. Example:

```scala
scala> numSet - 6
res12: scala.collection.immutable.Set[Int] =
  Set(5, 1, 2, 3, 4)
```

3. **++** : It adds a collection to a collection. Example:

```scala
scala> numSet ++ Set(6,7)
res16: scala.collection.immutable.Set[Int] =
  Set(5, 1, 6, 2, 7, 3, 4)
```

4. **- -** : It removes a collection from a set. Example:

```scala
scala> numSet -- Set(6,7)
res17: scala.collection.immutable.Set[Int] =
  Set(5, 1, 2, 3, 4)
```

5. *size* : It provides the size of a set. Example:

```scala
scala> numSet.size
res19: Int = 5
```

6. *contains* : It checks whether given element is present in a set. Example:

```
scala> numSet.contains(1)
res21: Boolean = true
```

More operations can be seen in the API documentation online. Please note that there are some operations specific to mutable sets.

12.3 Maps

Like sets, maps also come in two different flavors—immutable and mutable. A map is a structure whose elements are key-value pairs. In the code snippet below, we create a map of two countries, USA and Canada, with keys 1 and 2, respectively. Both the keys and values can be any objects.

```
scala> val countryMap = Map(1 -> "USA", 2 -> "Canada")
countryMap: scala.collection.immutable.Map[Int,String]
  = Map(1 -> USA, 2 -> Canada)
```

Next, let's look at some useful map operations.

1. + : It adds an entry to a map. Example.

```
scala> countryMap + (3 -> "UK")
res24: scala.collection.immutable.Map[Int,String] =
  Map(1 -> USA, 2 -> Canada, 3 -> UK)
```

2. - : It removes an entry from a map. We can remove an entry using its key. Example:

```
scala> countryMap - (3)
res26: scala.collection.immutable.Map[Int,String] =
  Map(1 -> USA, 2 -> Canada)
```

3. ++ : It adds another map or a collection to a map. Example:

```
scala> countryMap ++ Map(3 -> "UK", 4 -> "Japan")
res28: scala.collection.immutable.Map[Int,String] =
  Map(1 -> USA, 2 -> Canada, 3 -> UK, 4 -> Japan)
```

4. - - : It removes multiple entries. We can remove entries using the corresponding keys. Example:

```
scala> countryMap -- List(3,4)
res31: scala.collection.immutable.Map[Int,String] =
  Map(1 -> USA, 2 -> Canada)
```

5. *contains* : It returns a *Boolean value* if it finds a corresponding entry. Example:

```
scala> countryMap.contains(2)
res33: Boolean = true
```

6. *size* : It provides the size of a map. Example:

```
scala> countryMap.size
res34: Int = 2
```

7. <name of the map >(<key >) : It returns the corresponding value for the key. Example:

```
scala> countryMap(2)
res36: String = Canada
```

8. *isEmpty* : It returns true if a map is empty and returns false if a map is non-empty. Example:

```
scala> countryMap.isEmpty
res37: Boolean = false
```

9. *keys* : It returns all the keys of that map, as an *Iterable*. Example:

```
scala> countryMap.keys
res38: Iterable[Int] = Set(1, 2)
```

10. *keySet* : It returns keys as a set. Example:

```
scala> countryMap.keySet
res39: scala.collection.immutable.Set[Int] =
  Set(1, 2)
```

11. *values* : It returns all the values of a map, as an *Iterable*. Example:

```
scala> countryMap.values
res40: Iterable[String] = MapLike(USA, Canada)
```

12.4 Sequences

Sequences have indexed elements and inherit from the trait *Seq*. When a data structure is indexed, we can refer to each element by its index. Scala has numerous sequences and we discuss some of them here.

1. *List* : We discussed *List* details in Chapter 11. Lists are immutable and are widely used. Insertion and removal from the beginning of the list is fast, but this is not true for any arbitrary index.
2. *List Buffer* : As opposed to a *List*, a *ListBuffer* is mutable and performs in a constant time for both append as well as prepend. The operator += appends an item to a *ListBuffer* and +: prepends an item to a list buffer. Examples:

```
scala> val fruitBuffer = new ListBuffer[String]
fruitBuffer: scala.collection.mutable.
  ListBuffer[String] = ListBuffer()
```

```
scala> fruitBuffer += "apple"
res45: fruitBuffer.type = ListBuffer(apple)

scala> "mango" +: fruitBuffer
res46: scala.collection.mutable.ListBuffer[String]
 = ListBuffer(mango, apple)
```

3. *Array* : We have used *Array* before in this book. An array is a mutable data structure and is efficient in accessing an element at an arbitrary index. Just as a refresher, we create a couple of *Arrays* below. The first code snippet creates an array called *evenNums* and initializes it with even numbers below 10. The third code snippet creates an array called *oddNums* to hold odd numbers. The fourth code snippet shows how to insert an element in an array.

```
scala> val evenNums = Array(2,4,6,8)
evenNums: Array[Int] = Array(2, 4, 6, 8)

scala> evenNums(0)
res53: Int = 2

scala> val oddNums = new Array[Int](5)
oddNums: Array[Int] = Array(0, 0, 0, 0, 0)

scala> oddNums(0) = 1

scala> oddNums
res55: Array[Int] = Array(1, 0, 0, 0, 0)
```

4. *Array Buffer* : *ArrayBuffer* is a mutable data structure. In order to use it, we need to import *scala.collection.mutable.ArrayBuffer*. An *ArrayBuffer* is like an array with additional append and prepend operations. Also elements can be removed from the beginning as well as from the end. Examples:

```
scala> import scala.collection.mutable.ArrayBuffer
import scala.collection.mutable.ArrayBuffer

scala> val fruitBuff = new ArrayBuffer[String]()
fruitBuff: scala.collection.mutable.
 ArrayBuffer[String] = ArrayBuffer()

scala> fruitBuff += "apple"
res56: fruitBuff.type = ArrayBuffer(apple)

scala> fruitBuff.length
res58: Int = 1
```

5. *Stack* : Stack is available both as an immutable as well as a mutable data structure in Scala. This is a classical data structure in computer science that simulates last-in-first-out activities of the real world. Let's look at some common operations on Stack. The examples are self-explanatory.

```scala
scala> import scala.collection.mutable.Stack
import scala.collection.mutable.Stack

scala> val stackSim = new Stack[String]
stackSim: scala.collection.mutable.Stack[String]
 = Stack()

scala> stackSim.push("Scala Book")
res60: stackSim.type = Stack(Scala Book)

scala> stackSim.push("Java Book")
res61: stackSim.type = Stack(Java Book, Scala Book)

scala> stackSim
res62: scala.collection.mutable.Stack[String] =
Stack(Java Book, Scala Book)

scala> stackSim.top
res66: String = Java Book

scala> stackSim.pop
res69: String = Java Book

scala> stackSim
res70: scala.collection.mutable.Stack[String] =
Stack(Scala Book)
```

6. *Queue* : Like stack, queue is also available both as an immutable and a mutable data structure, and simulates first-in-first-out activities of the real world. The code snippets below present several common queue operations.

```scala
scala> import scala.collection.mutable.Queue
import scala.collection.mutable.Queue

scala> val queueSim = new Queue[Int]
queueSim: scala.collection.mutable.Queue[Int]
 = Queue()

scala> queueSim += 1
res72: queueSim.type = Queue(1)
```

```
scala> queueSim ++= List(3,5)
res73: queueSim.type = Queue(1, 3, 5)

scala> queueSim.dequeue
res74: Int = 1

scala> queueSim
res75: scala.collection.mutable.Queue[Int] =
  Queue(3, 5)

scala> queueSim.enqueue(1)

scala> queueSim
res77: scala.collection.mutable.Queue[Int] =
  Queue(3, 5, 1)
```

12.5 Tuples

A tuple combines multiple items into one group so that multiple items could be processed as one item. When it groups, it doesn't lose the identity of an individual item so that the item can be extracted and processed individually. A tuple can be a handy feature to represent certain combinations, which don't have to be necessarily expressed using classes. So it is the developer who decides which one models the given situation better. Tuples are immutable and can hold objects of different types. Scala can infer the type of a tuple based on its elements.

The following code snippet creates a tuple containing two elements. Since the type of both the elements is String, the type of tuple is (String, String). The first element of the tuple is accessed by writing the tuple name followed by a dot, which is followed by an underscore and 1, as shown in the code snippet below. Similarly, the second element can be accessed with 2 and so on. The number here looks more like a subscript. Please note that the index starts from 1, not from 0.

```
scala> val statePair = ("CA", "California")
statePair: (String, String) = (CA,California)

scala> statePair._1
res78: String = CA

scala> statePair._2
res79: String = California
```

As far as assignment is concerned, a tuple can be treated as a single unit. For example, in the following code snippet, we have assigned tuple (1,2) to tuple (a,b). The first identifier of the target gets the first element of the source and so on. Next, we've treated the tuple elements as individual variables and performed an addition.

```scala
scala> val (a,b) = (1,2)
a: Int = 1
b: Int = 2

scala> a + b
res81: Int = 3
```

12.6 Conclusion

In this chapter, we discussed mutable and immutable collections. Mutable collections provide convenience for program reasoning. Next, we discussed sets and related operations. Scala sets are like mathematical sets and contain unique elements. Then we covered maps, which are key-value pairs. Next, we discussed different types of sequences—list, list buffer, array, array buffer, stack, and queue. Finally, we discussed tuples.

12.7 Review Questions

1. What is a major difference between a mutable collection and an immutable collection?
2. What is the output of the following code snippet? The auto-generated identifier may not match, which is expected.

   ```scala
   scala> val nums = Set(10,11,12,15)
   nums: scala.collection.immutable.Set[Int] =
     Set(10, 11, 12, 15)

   scala> nums - 15
   ```

3. What is the output of the following code snippet? Please note that *nums* was defined in the previous question.

   ```scala
   scala> nums -- Set(10,11)
   ```

4. What is the output of the following code snippet?

   ```scala
   scala> nums
   ```

5. What is the output of the following code snippet?

```scala
scala> val westCities =
  Map(1 -> "San Jose", 2 -> "Palo Alto")
westCities: scala.collection.immutable.Map[Int,String]
  = Map(1 -> San Jose, 2 -> Palo Alto)

scala> val eastCities =
  Map(1 -> "Boston", 2 -> "New York")
eastCities: scala.collection.immutable.
  Map[Int,String] = Map(1 -> Boston, 2 -> New York)

scala> westCities.contains(1) ==
  eastCities.contains(1)
```

6. What is the output of the following code snippet?

```scala
scala> westCities -- List(1,2)
res88: scala.collection.immutable.Map[Int,String]
  = Map()

scala> westCities
```

7. What is the output of the following code snippet?

```scala
scala> val num = new ListBuffer[Int]
num: scala.collection.mutable.ListBuffer[Int]
  = ListBuffer()

scala> num += 2
res90: num.type = ListBuffer(2)

scala> num(0)
```

8. What is the output of the following code snippet?

```scala
scala> val ranStack = new Stack[Int]
ranStack: scala.collection.mutable.Stack[Int]
  = Stack()

scala> ranStack.push(2).push(3)
res96: ranStack.type = Stack(3, 2)

scala> ranStack.pop
```

9. What is the output of the following code snippet?

```scala
scala> val ranQueue = new Queue[Int]
ranQueue: scala.collection.mutable.Queue[Int]
  = Queue()
```

```
scala> ranQueue.enqueue(2)

scala> ranQueue.enqueue(1)

scala> ranQueue.dequeue
```

10. What is the output of the following code snippet?

```
scala> val ranTuple = ("pi", 3.1416)
ranTuple: (String, Double) = (pi,3.1416)

scala> val dumTuple =("mi", 2.1416)
dumTuple: (String, Double) = (mi,2.1416)

scala> ranTuple._2 == dumTuple._2
```

12.8 Problems

1. Assume that there are two baskets—A and B. Basket A was shipped from Mexico to USA and basket B was shipped from China to USA. In order to reduce the shipping cost, the fruits were mixed and shipped in one basket, i.e., both the baskets have apples as well as oranges. Each fruit item is labeled uniquely. For example, an apple from China is labeled as CA1 and an apple from Mexico is labeled as MA1. Each student is given exactly one apple and one orange. Using set, write a program to calculate the maximum number of students that can be served by basket A and basket B. You can create sample data, with hard coded values.

2. Assume that data center A has a map containing 3 key-value pairs and data center B has a map containing 2 key-value pairs. Each key-value pair represents an available virtual box; a key represents an id and a value represents a capacity. Write a program to select the last virtual box from the combined map of virtual boxes. Hard coded sample data is fine to solve this problem.

3. Write a program to remove the last virtual box from the context of the previous problem and to find a virtual box with the highest capacity.

12.9 Answers to Review Questions

1. A mutable collection can be re-assigned but an immutable collection cannot be re-assigned.

2. res82: scala.collection.immutable.Set[Int] = Set(10, 11, 12). (Note: your auto-generated identifier can be different.)

3. res83: scala.collection.immutable.Set[Int] = Set(12, 15)
4. res84: scala.collection.immutable.Set[Int] = Set(10, 11, 12, 15)
5. true
6. res89: scala.collection.immutable.Map[Int,String] = Map(1 -> San Jose, 2 -> Palo Alto)
7. res95: Int = 2
8. res99: Int = 3
9. res104: Int = 2
10. res105: Boolean = false

12.10 Solutions to Problems

```scala
1. object BasketApp {
      def main(args: Array[String]): Unit = {
         val basketA =
          Set("CA1","CA2","CA3","CO1","CO2","CO3","CO4")
         val basketB =
          Set("MA1","MA2","MA3","MA4","MO1","MO2","MO3")

         def findServInA(x: Set[String]): (Int,Int) = {
            var appCount = 0
            var oraCount = 0
            for(elem <- x) {
               if (elem.startsWith("CA")) {
                  appCount += 1
               } else if(elem.startsWith("CO")) {
                  oraCount += 1
               }
            }
            (appCount,oraCount)
         }

         def findServInB(y: Set[String]): (Int,Int) = {
            var appCount = 0
            var oraCount = 0
            for(elem <- y) {
               if (elem.startsWith("MA")) {
                  appCount += 1
               } else if(elem.startsWith("MO")) {
                  oraCount += 1
               }
            }
            (appCount,oraCount)
         }

         val (chinaApp, chinaOra) = findServInA(basketA)
         val (mexApp, mexOra) = findServInB(basketB)

         val totalApples = chinaApp + mexApp
         val totalOranges = chinaOra + mexOra
         val servRef = if (totalApples < totalOranges) totalApples
          else totalOranges

         println("Max. students that can be served = " + servRef)

      }
   }

2. object DataCenterApp1 {
      def main(args: Array[String]): Unit = {
         val datcen1 = Map(1 -> 234, 2 -> 100, 3 -> 400)
         val datcen2 = Map(100 -> 200, 101 -> 1024)
         val combDataCenter = datcen1 ++ datcen2
         println(combDataCenter.toList.last)
      }
   }
```

3.
```scala
object DataCenterApp2 {
   def main(args: Array[String]): Unit = {
      val dataCenter1 = Map(1 -> 234, 2 -> 100, 3 -> 400)
      val dataCenter2 = Map(100 -> 200, 101 -> 1024)
      val combDataCenter = dataCenter1 ++ dataCenter2
      val lastElemAsList = combDataCenter.toList.last
      val refreshedDataCenter = combDataCenter --
        List(lastElemAsList._1)
      val maxCapacityValue = refreshedDataCenter.values.max
      println("Highest capacity virtual box id is "+
        keyForValue(refreshedDataCenter, maxCapacityValue))
   }

   def keyForValue(aMap: Map[Int,Int], aValue: Int): Int = {
      val aList = aMap.toList
      var aKey = 0
      for(elem <- aList) {
         if(elem._2 == aValue) {
            aKey = elem._1
         }
      }
      aKey
   }
}
```

Chapter 13
Actors

The actor model of computation has a long history [HBS73]. It is an interesting model of computation in the sense that each actor is like a human agent that is capable of receiving, processing, and sending messages. Also the actor model provides a hierarchy of actors so that work can be divided or can be delegated. This makes the system fault tolerant, because if one actor dies, the work can be assigned to another actor.

Scala actors pass immutable messages so as to enable better program reasoning. Originally the actor library was a part of Scala and later it transitioned to the Akka actor library. The transition allows the actor library to evolve as a separate module, as it is a significant computational module. There are programming languages primarily based on the actor model of computation, including Erlang. For the purpose of our discussions, please include something equivalent to *libraryDependencies +=* *"com.typesafe.akka" %% "akka-actor" % "2.5.1"* in your build.sbt file, if you are using an SBT project in an IDE. At the time of writing, version 2.5.1 was the latest stable release of the Akka toolkit.

13.1 The Components of Actors

In order to write a simple custom actor, all we need to do is write a class that extends the trait *Actor* and implement the *receive* method. The remaining things are taken care of by the framework itself. In Figure 13.1, the class *SimpleActor* extends the trait *Actor*. This trait has numerous methods; we will be discussing some of these later in this chapter. *receive* is the only method that is required in order to recognize the class as an actor.

© Springer International Publishing AG 2017
B.P. Upadhyaya, *Programming with Scala*, Undergraduate
Topics in Computer Science, https://doi.org/10.1007/978-3-319-69368-2_13

```
import akka.actor.{Props, ActorSystem, Actor}
class SimpleActor extends Actor {
   def receive = {
      case "Scala" => println("Scala programming")
      case "Java" => println("Java programming")
      case _ => println("No match found")
   }
}

object SampleActorApp {
   def main(args: Array[String]): Unit = {
      val actorSystem = ActorSystem("SampleActorSystem")
      val simpleActor = actorSystem.actorOf(Props[SimpleActor],
       name = "simActor")
      simpleActor ! "Scala"
      simpleActor ! "Java"
      simpleActor ! "Erlang"
   }
}
```

Fig. 13.1: Simple Actor

13.2 Creating Actors

In order to create an actor, we need to create an *ActorSystem*, which has necessary methods that allow us to create and manage actors. Also it is common practice to create one *ActorSystem* per application. We supply a name to *ActorSystem* so that it can be referred, as shown in Figure 13.1. *ActorSystem* is responsible for allocating one or more threads for our application. This is one of the advantages of the Akka toolkit over low level threads oriented programming, like Java multi-threaded programming.

Once we have an instance of *ActorSystem*, we can use its *actorOf* operation to create an actor. We supply two arguments—*Props* of *SimpleActor* and a name to our actor. Please note that *SimpleActor* is the class we defined and *Props* is part of the Akka toolkit, which contains necessary members to make *SimpleActor* an actor, including *mailbox, routerConfig*, and *dispatcher*.

If we look at the signature of *actorOf, def actorOf(props : akka.actor.Props, name : scala.Predef.String) : akka.actor.ActorRef*, we find that it returns an instance of *ActorRef*, which is a handle to the actor. When we call the operation *actorOf*, an actor is started asynchronously. *ActorRef* is more like an interface between a programmer and the actual actor. *ActorRef* is serializable, immutable, and network aware. Also it has a one-to-one relationship with the actor, *SimpleActor* in our case.

13.3 Sending and Receiving Messages

Communication with actors is done through message passing. Figure 13.2 presents a typical message passing between two actors and a driver program. It has two actors—*BankOfAmerica* and *Chase*, which communicate with each other for the purpose of account validation. The driver program creates two actors called *boa* and *chase*. When the *chase* actor is created, an actor reference to *boa* is passed, which enables direct message passing from *chase* to *boa*.

Once the actors are created, the message *deposit* is passed to the actor *chase*, which matches with the *case "deposit"*, which causes the code in this case to be executed. The last line of code sends the message *deposit-complete* to the actor *boa*. This matches with the *case "deposit-complete"*, which sets the flag and prints *Ready for debit*. From the user's perspective, this chain of communication ends here.

Next, the message *debit* is sent to the actor *chase*. If the *depositCompleted* flag is set to true, it will print the message *Debit completed*, on the console. In the next LOC, it passes the message *debit-complete* to the actor *boa*. There is a corresponding case to handle this message, which first checks whether the *depositComplete* flag is set to true. If it is set to true, it will print the message *Process completed*, on the console. The order of the messages printed on the console may be different in different run, because the communication is an asynchronous process.

```scala
import akka.actor.{ActorRef, Props, ActorSystem, Actor}
class BankOfAmerica extends Actor {
   var depositComplete = false
   def receive = {
      case "deposit-complete" => {
         depositComplete = true
         println("Ready for debit")
      }
      case "debit-complete" => {
         if(depositComplete == true) {
            println("Process completed")
         }
      }
      case _ => println("Unknown status")
   }
}
class Chase(boa: ActorRef) extends Actor {
   var depositCompleted = true
   def receive = {
      case "deposit" => {
         depositCompleted = true
         println("Deposit complete")
         boa ! "deposit-complete"
      }
      case "debit" => {
         if(depositCompleted == true) {
            println("Debit completed")
            boa ! "debit-complete"
         }
      }
      case _ => println("Unknown status")
   }
}
object MessageExchangeActorApp {
   def main(args: Array[String]): Unit = {
      val actorSystem = ActorSystem("AccountVerification")
      val boa =
       actorSystem.actorOf(Props[BankOfAmerica],"boa-actor")
      val chase = actorSystem.actorOf(Props(new Chase(boa)),
       "chase-actor")
      chase ! "deposit"
      chase ! "debit"
   }
}
```

Fig. 13.2: Sending and Receiving Messages

13.4 Life Cycle

The actor life cycle starts when an actor is created and the life cycle can be understood through life cycle related methods:

- *preStart* : This method is called as soon as an actor is started and is called before the *receive* method is called.
- *receive* : As the name suggests, it receives messages and processes them.
- *postStop* : It is called after an actor is stopped and can be used for cleanup. For example, if an actor is closely tied with a database connection, that connection can be closed as a part of post operations.
- *preRestart* : It is called before an actor is restarted and is used to inform what caused the restart. It takes an exception and a message as parameters; the exception is the cause of restart and there might be a message that caused that exception.
- *postRestart* : It is called immediately after an actor is restarted and takes an exception that caused the restart as its parameter.

Figure 13.3 overrides actor life cycle methods to show when they are called. All of these methods have at least one line of code that prints on the console so that we can compare messages and see the order of invocation. The output for this program is as shown below.

```
CarActor constructor
CarActor: preStart
Some message
CarActor: preRestart
Cause: Force restart
Message: ForceRestart
CarActor constructor
CarActor: postRestart
Cause: Force restart
[ERROR] [06/08/2017 19:05:30.459] [Actor...
java.lang.Exception: Force restart
...
Terminating actor system
CarActor: postStop

Process finished with exit code 0
```

Please note that the method *postStop* was not called when the actor *carActor* was restarted. The method *receive* is more like the body of the actor and was invoked after *preStart*. When we created an artificial exception, the actor was restarted automatically. We did not explicitly pass the exception or the message, but those were captured by the toolkit.

```scala
import akka.actor.{Props, ActorSystem, Actor}
case object ForceRestart
class CarActor extends Actor {
   println("CarActor constructor")
   override def preStart: Unit = {
      println("CarActor: preStart")
   }
   override def postStop: Unit = {
      println("CarActor: postStop")
   }
   override def preRestart(cause: Throwable,
    message: Option[Any]): Unit = {
      println("CarActor: preRestart")
      println(s" Cause: ${cause.getMessage}")
      println(s" Message: ${message.getOrElse("None")}")
   }
   override def postRestart(cause: Throwable): Unit ={
      println("CarActor: postRestart")
      println(s" Cause: ${cause.getMessage}")
   }
   def receive = {
      case ForceRestart => throw new Exception("Force restart")
      case _ => println("Some message")
   }
}
object ActorLifecycleApp {
   def main(args: Array[String]): Unit = {
      val actorSystem = ActorSystem("ActorLifeCycle")
      val carActor = actorSystem.actorOf(Props[CarActor], name
       = "car")

      carActor ! "first message"
      Thread.sleep(2000)
      carActor ! ForceRestart
      Thread.sleep(2000)
      actorSystem.stop(carActor)
      println("Terminating actor system")
      actorSystem.terminate()
   }
}
```

Fig. 13.3: Actor Life Cycle

13.5 Child Actors

The actor model of computation is an interesting computing paradigm. For the purpose of analysis, let's take an example of an organization. An organization has a president or CEO. There can be multiple vice presidents, as each of them will be looking after a specific aspect of business like finance, engineering, operations, etc.

When a big task is assigned to the organization, it is assigned to the CEO. But it is not the CEO who does all the work.

The CEO breaks down the task in terms of organization segments; these segments are responsible for a particular type of task. Next, the CEO delegates tasks to vice presidents, based on their expertise. Vice presidents break down the tasks and delegate to their sub-ordinates, who could be senior directors. Now the senior directors may break down the task and delegate to the next level. This continues until it reaches the working level. Actor hierarchy is similar to this context.

Figure 13.4 presents two actors *President* and *VicePresident*. We have a couple of case classes to help create actors. In the actor *President*, we have a case to create an actor of type *VicePresident*. From the driver program, when a message of type *CreateVicePresident* is sent, it matches with the first case in the *President* actor's *receive* method. In the first case, an actor of type *VicePresident* is created. Please note that we use *context*, which is of type *ActorContext*, when we create a child actor from a parent actor. This is different from when we create an actor from the driver program, which uses *ActorSystem*.

The name passed as a parameter to the message of type *CreateVicePresident* is assigned to the identifier *name*. Please note the prefix *s*; this allows us to write expressions inside double quotes, which eventually evaluate to a string value before assignment is made. The *name* after the dollar sign indicates an identifier, not a literal value. In the next LOC, an object *Name* with a parameter *name* is passed to the newly created actor *vp*. In the corresponding case within the *VicePresident* actor, there is only assignment, so nothing is printed on the console.

Next, the actor *vp* is passed a message *hello*, which matches with the default case in the *VicePresident* actor that causes the corresponding string to be printed, on the console. Please note that this string also has an identifier, which has a default value *None*. We have overridden the *postStop* method so that we can see an output on the console, when an actor of type *VicePresident* is terminated.

On the driver program side, the actor *president* gets a message of type *CreateVicePresident*, which is parameterized. We have already discussed the corresponding case, in the *President* actor, for this. This creates a *VicePresident* actor. Next, we select that vice president actor using *actorSelection*. Please note how names and the URL-like structure are related. The names that we provided during actor creation can be used to locate the actor. Also please note that the child actor is within the parent actor in the URL-like structure. Next, we kill the vice president actor by passing *PoisonPill*. *PoisonPill* is a case object provided by the Akka toolkit. When we pass it as a message to an actor, it kills that actor. Finally, we wait for a second and then terminate the actor system.

```scala
import akka.actor._
case class Name(name: String)
case class CreateVicePresident(name: String)
class President extends Actor {
   def receive = {
      case CreateVicePresident(name) => {
         val vp = context.actorOf(Props[VicePresident],
          name = s"$name")
         vp ! Name(name)
         vp ! "hello"
      }
      case _ => println("President got a message")
   }
}
class VicePresident extends Actor {
   var name = "None"
   def receive = {
      case Name(name) => this.name = name
      case _ =>
       println(s"Vice president, $name, got a message")
   }
   override def postStop: Unit = {
      println(s"I, $name, got stopped")
   }
}

object ChildActorsApp {
   def main(args: Array[String]): Unit = {
      val actorSystem = ActorSystem("ChildActorSystem")
      val president = actorSystem.
       actorOf(Props[President], name = "President")
      president ! CreateVicePresident("Hilbert")
      Thread.sleep(1000)

      val hilbert = actorSystem.actorSelection(
       "/user/President/Hilbert")
      hilbert ! PoisonPill
      Thread.sleep(1000)
      actorSystem.terminate()
   }
}
```

Fig. 13.4: Child Actors

13.6 Monitoring

The ability to know whether sub-ordinate actors are functional is important as work is delegated to sub-ordinate actors, also known as child actors. The Akka framework provides features so that a parent actor can automatically detect when a child actor is stopped. When a parent actor calls the *watch* operation on *context*, the parent is notified when a child actor is dead.

Figure 13.5 has two actors—*Developer* and *Manager*. *Manager* is the parent actor and is responsible for creating a *Developer* actor. *Manager* can watch the *Developer* actor by calling *watch* on *context*. The *watch* operation takes a child actor as its parameter, *developer* in this case. When *developer* is killed, the message *Manager* receives matches with the case *Terminated(developer)*.

Now, let's look at the driver program. After creating the actor system, we create a *Manager* actor, *manager*. Since the child actor creation is part of the constructor code, *developer* actor is created when *manager* actor is created. Also developer watch is created during the creation process. Next, we select *Developer* and pass *PoisonPill* to it so that it is killed. When *Developer* is terminated, the *Terminated(developer)* case of *Manager* holds true and the corresponding code is executed. So it is evident that the supervisor or the parent actor is aware when its sub-ordinate actor is no longer functional. This is how it knows when to delegate the task to some other sub-ordinate actors, in case of failure. In other words, this feature makes it practical to develop fault-tolerant systems.

```scala
import akka.actor._

class Developer extends Actor {
    def receive = {
        case "start" => println("Developer started working")
        case _ => println("Developer received a message")
    }
}

class Manager extends Actor {
    val developer = context.actorOf(Props[Developer], name =
    "Developer")
    developer ! "start"
    context.watch(developer)

    def receive = {
        case Terminated(developer) =>
         println("Developer got poison pill")
        case _ => println("Manager received a messsage")
    }
}

object ActorMonitoringApp {
    def main(args: Array[String]): Unit = {
        val actorSystem = ActorSystem("Management")
        val manager = actorSystem.actorOf(Props[Manager], name =
         "Manager")

        val dev =
         actorSystem.actorSelection("/user/Manager/Developer")
        dev ! PoisonPill
        Thread.sleep(3000)
        actorSystem.terminate()
    }
}
```

Fig. 13.5: Actor Monitoring

13.7 Conclusion

In this chapter, we started with the basic components of an actor and then demonstrated how to create actors. Actors communicate with each other by sending and receiving messages. Also driver programs and the framework communicate with the help of messages. We presented a detailed example for sending and receiving messages. Next, we covered important life cycle methods. Tracking the messages from these methods is an important aspect of actor management. Further, we discussed how to create and manage child actors, an important aspect of hierarchical actors. Finally, we discussed actor monitoring.

13.8 Review Questions

1. Write one major difference between the object model of computation and the actor model of computation.
2. Write one major difference between the functional model of computation and the actor model of computation.
3. As of Akka version 2.5.1, what is one mandatory method that we need to implement in order to make a class an actor?
4. Which class is used to create an actor system?
5. In order for the following code snippet to work, what actor class is required?

```
val actorSystem = ActorSystem("University")
val admin = actorSystem.actorOf(
  Props[Administrator], name = "Admin")
```

6. Describe a circumstance which requires the following type of code snippet in order to create an actor.

```
val myActor = context.actorOf(Props[MyActor],
  name = "myAct")
```

7. In *chem ! PoisonPill*, what is the name of the actor? What is the use of *PoisonPill*?
8. Is the *PoisonPill* a system defined object?
9. In the following code snippet, what is the name of the actor that we are trying to select?

```
val actorSystem = ActorSystem("UniversitySys")
val findChild = actorSystem.
 actorSelection("/user/University/Professor")
```

10. In the following code snippet, what is $name?

```
val vp = context.actorOf(Props[VicePresident],
  name = s"$name")
```

11. Write a code snippet that watches a child actor called *tester*.

13.9 Problems

1. Implement an actor called *Instructor*, which adds a student to a common list of students, when it receives a message of type *Student*. Make necessary assumptions and choices in order to create a realistic solution.
2. Implement an actor called *TeachingAsst* that can delegate the course registration task from the actor *Instructor* implemented for the previous problem. Next, modify the actor *Instructor* so that it creates a teaching assistant as its child actor. In addition to this, create one more teaching assistant child actor, which is responsible for registering teaching materials. Delegate the tasks appropriately. Also

include code to watch the child actors. Make realistic assumptions to solve the problem.

3. Write a driver program for the actors implemented for the previous two problems. Pass necessary sample messages to demonstrate course registration and teaching material registration. Also add case classes, if needed.

13.10 Answers to Review Questions

1. The object model of computation models real world objects with programming language objects. The actor model of computation models real world actors with programming language actors.
2. The functional model of computation models computational elements with functions. For example, algorithms can be embedded in a function. The actor model of computation represents real world agents with programming language actors.
3. As of Akka version 2.5.1, the one method that is mandatory to make a class an actor is *receive*.
4. The class *ActorSystem* is used to create an actor system.
5. In order for the code snippet to work, we need an actor class called *Administrator*.
6. We use *context*, which is of type *akka.actor.ActorContext*, in order to create a child actor from within a parent actor.
7. *chem* is the name of an actor. When we send a message *PoisonPill* to an actor, it terminates that actor.
8. Yes, *PoisonPill* is part of the Akka toolkit and it is a case object.
9. *Professor* is the name of the actor that we are trying to select.
10. $name inside double quotes means it is an identifier, which can be replaced by a corresponding value. Eventually, the expression, *s"$name"*, forms a string.
11. *context.watch(tester)*

13.11 Solutions to Problems

1.
```scala
import akka.actor.Actor
import scala.collection.mutable.ArrayBuffer

case class Student(name: String, course: String)

class Instructor extends Actor {
   var allStudents = new ArrayBuffer[Student]()
   def receive = {
      case student @ Student(x,y) => {
         allStudents.append(student)
      }
      case _ => println("Unknown message")
   }
}
```

2.
```scala
import akka.actor.{Actor, Props}
import scala.collection.mutable.ArrayBuffer

case class Student(name: String, course: String)

case class Material(courseName: String, materialID: String)

class Instructor extends Actor {
   val hari =
    context.actorOf(Props[TeachingAsst], name = "Hari")
   val sam = context.actorOf(Props[TeachingAsst], name = "Sam")
   context.watch(hari)
   context.watch(sam)

   def receive = {
      case Student(x,y) => {
         hari ! Student(x,y)
      }
      case Material(x,y) => {
         sam ! Material(x,y)
      }
      case _ => println("Instructor got a message")
   }
}

class TeachingAsst extends Actor {
   var allStudents = new ArrayBuffer[Student]()
   var allMaterials = new ArrayBuffer[Material]()

   def receive = {
      case student @ Student(x,y) => {
         allStudents.append(student)
      }
      case material @ Material(x,y) => {
         allMaterials.append(material)
      }
      case _ => println("TA got a message")
   }
}
```

3.
```scala
import akka.actor.{ActorSystem, Props}

object InstructorActorApp {
  def main(args: Array[String]): Unit = {
    val actorSystem = ActorSystem("InstructorActSystem")
    val instructor = actorSystem.actorOf(Props[Instructor],
     name = "instructor")

    instructor ! Student("Newton", "Physics")
    instructor ! Student("Darwin", "Biology")
    instructor ! Student("Rutherford", "Chemistry")

    instructor ! Material("Physics", "Lect1")
    instructor ! Material("Biology", "Lect1")
    instructor ! Material("Chemistry", "Lect1")

    Thread.sleep(1000)
    actorSystem.terminate()
  }
}
```

Chapter 14
XML Processing

XML is a common way of structuring data for Internet based applications. If you are part of a team that develops web applications, then it is highly likely that you will encounter XML in some way. It is a common requirement to convert raw data to XML and vice-versa. Raw data might come from databases, might be generated from within the application using programs, etc. In any case, it is helpful to be equipped with tools that allow us to process XML.

Scala supports XML processing through its XML module. If you are using Scala REPL, you can simply import required classes. If you are using an IDE and an SBT based project, then you need to include a required dependency so that the corresponding jar file is fetched. A typical dependency entry in the *build.sbt* file looks like *libraryDependencies += "org.scala-lang" % "scala-xml" % "2.11.0-M4"*. Please note that the version might differ depending upon what version you would like to work with. Also the double quotes will look different in your editor. You can simply use the double quotes available on your keyboard.

14.1 XML Literals

In Scala, XML processing can be done as if it is a language core feature. We can use XML as a literal to form a valid expression. For example, in the following code snippet, we have <fruit > as a tag and *apple* as a value. The type of this expression is *scala.xml.Elem*.

```
scala> <fruit> apple </fruit>
res1: scala.xml.Elem = <fruit> apple </fruit>
```

Now, let's take one more example to illustrate how embedded tags are interpreted. The code snippet below defines an XML element *person* that has two child elements—*fName* and *lName*. Scala interprets it like an embedded XML structure.

```
scala> val person =
```

© Springer International Publishing AG 2017
B.P. Upadhyaya, *Programming with Scala*, Undergraduate
Topics in Computer Science, https://doi.org/10.1007/978-3-319-69368-2_14

```
<person>
 <fName>Charles</fName>
 <lName>Darwin</lName>
</person>
person: scala.xml.Elem =
 <person><fName>Charles</fName>
 <lName>Darwin</lName></person>
```

The *scala.xml* package has numerous classes and objects to process XML. Here we list some of these, along with their definitions from the Scala API documentation.

- *Seq[Node]* : It is a sequence of type *Node*.
- *NodeSeq* : It implements a wrapper around *Seq[Node]*, which adds XPath and comprehension methods.
- *Document* : It represents a document information item.
- *Node* : It is an abstract class that represents XML with nodes of labelled trees. Also it contains implementation for subsets of XPath for navigation purposes. It is an abstract superclass of all XML node classes.
- *Elem* : It provides an immutable data object representing an XML node. It extends the *Node* class.
- *Group* : It is used to group XML nodes in one node for output.
- *SpecialNode* : It is a special XML node that represents either text (PCDATA), a comment, or an entity reference.
- *Atom* : It provides an XML node for text (PCDATA).
- *EntityRef* : It implements an XML node for entity reference.
- *ProcInstr* : It provides an XML node for processing instructions.
- *Comment* : It implements an XML node for comments.
- *Text* : It implements an XML node for text (PCDATA). For example, *Charles* in *<firstName > Charles </firstName >* is of type *Text*.
- *PCData* : It represents parseable character data.
- *Unparsed* : It represents an XML node for unparsed content.

Scala gives developers more power by allowing them to write Scala code within an XML tag. Figure 14.1 has two occurrences of *val* representing first name and last name. Next, it defines an XML structure to represent names. The corresponding identifiers can be placed within the tags to pull values. Please note the curly braces; the content inside curly braces is evaluated. So we can put Scala code inside the curly braces. This allows processing logic to be placed inside the tags.

The output for the program in Figure 14.1 is as shown below. *firstName* was replaced by "Isaac" and *secondName* was replaced by "Newton". When we work as professional programmers in industry, we encounter many business needs that require us to generate XML tags. Many business-to-business (B2B) communications happen with XML exchanges. So this feature is a handy feature for developers solving real world software engineering problems.

```
object MixingXMLAndScalaApp {
    def main(args: Array[String]): Unit = {
        val firstName = "Isaac"
        val lastName = "Newton"

        val myXML =
         <name>
          <firstName>{firstName}</firstName>
          <lastName>{lastName}</lastName>
         </name>

        println(myXML)
    }
}
```

Fig. 14.1: XML with Scala Code

```
<name>
 <firstName>Isaac</firstName>
 <lastName>Newton</lastName>
</name>
```

The code snippet belows shows a tag *sum*. Within this tag, we have an arithmetic expression. When this tag is processed, the expression within curly braces is evaluated and hence we get the result, 5.

```
scala> <sum>{2+3}</sum>
res2: scala.xml.Elem = <sum>5</sum>
```

14.2 Data Extraction

Once we receive XML, we need to extract data so that further action can be taken. Scala provides numerous operations to extract data from an XML input. We don't have to bother too much about the structure of XML in order to extract data. We present some of the most useful operations below.

- Text Extraction *(text)* : The text within a tag can be extracted using the *text* operation. The code snippet below has one tag *cityName* and has "Sunnyvale" as a value. When we call the *text* operation on the XML, we get the value "Sunnyvale".

  ```
  scala> <cityName>Sunnyvale</cityName>.text
  res3: String = Sunnyvale
  ```

- Label Extraction *(label)* : The tag label can be extracted using the *label* operation, as shown in the code snippet below.

```
scala> <cityName>Sunnyvale</cityName>.label
res4: String = cityNam
```

- Searching Immediate Child Nodes (\) : The immediate child nodes can be
  searched using a single back slash (\). The code snippet below extracts all the
  immediate child nodes with label *p*.

```
scala> <html><p>San Jose</p><p>Sunnyvale<a>warm</a>
</p> </html> \ "p"
res5: scala.xml.NodeSeq = NodeSeq(<p>San Jose</p>,
<p>Sunnyvale<a>warm</a></p>)
```

- Searching Any Depth (\\) : The child nodes can be searched at any depth using
  double back slashes (\\). The code snippet below searches all the child nodes, at
  any depth, with label *a*.

```
scala> <html><p>San Jose</p><p>Sunnyvale<a>warm</a>
</p> </html> \\ "a"
res7: scala.xml.NodeSeq = NodeSeq(<a>warm</a>)
```

- Attribute Value Extraction *(attribute(<attribute name >))* : An attribute value
  can be extracted by passing an attribute name to either the *attribute* or *attributes*
  operation, as shown below.

```
scala> <a href="https://www.w3schools.com">
This is a link</a>.attribute("href")
res8: Option[Seq[scala.xml.Node]] =
Some(https://www.w3schools.com)

scala> <a href="https://www.w3schools.com">
This is a link</a>.attributes("href")
res9: Seq[scala.xml.Node] =
https://www.w3schools.com
```

- Attribute Values Processing : This is an elaboration of the previous operation,
  attributes. The attributes can be extracted as keys and values. Also the attributes
  can be extracted as a map.

```
scala> val xmlData = <stock day="Mon"
date="Jun 14 2017"
low="103" high="105" />
xmlData: scala.xml.Elem = <stock day="Mon"
date="Jun 14 2017"
low="103" high="105"/>

scala> xmlData.attributes
res10: scala.xml.MetaData =  day="Mon"
date="Jun 14 2017"
```

```
  low="103" high="105"

scala> for(att <- xmlData.attributes)
 println(s"key: ${att.key}, value: ${att.value}")
key: day, value: Mon
key: date, value: Jun 14 2017
key: low, value: 103
key: high, value: 105

scala> xmlData.attributes.asAttrMap
res12: Map[String,String] = Map(day -> Mon,
 date -> Jun 14 2017,
 low -> 103, high -> 105)
```

- Child Nodes Extraction *(child)* : Child nodes can be extracted using the *child* operation, as shown below.

```
scala> val cityData =   <city><name>Sunnyvale</name>
 <state>CA</state></city>
cityData: scala.xml.Elem = <city>
 <name>Sunnyvale</name>
 <state>CA</state></city>

scala> cityData.child
res13: Seq[scala.xml.Node] =
 ArrayBuffer(<name>Sunnyvale</name>,
 <state>CA</state>)

scala> for(a <- cityData.child) println(a)
<name>Sunnyvale</name>
<state>CA</state>

scala> for(a <- cityData.child) yield a.text
res18: Seq[String] = ArrayBuffer(Sunnyvale, CA)

scala> cityData.child(1)
res15: scala.xml.Node = <state>CA</state>

scala> cityData.child(1).label
res16: String = state

scala> cityData.child(1).text
res17: String = CA
```

- String Conversion *(toString)* : It converts an XML structure to a string.

```
scala> cityData.toString
```

```
res20: String = <city><name>Sunnyvale</name>
<state>CA</state></city>
```

Scala allows deep XML searching using XPath expressions. Also there are many other operations which can be used to process XML. In this volume, we aim for content that gives a good start.

14.3 Pattern Matching

We demonstrated an example of XML pattern matching in Section 10.10, page 120. In this section, we cover an additional method. When one or more child nodes is present, the pattern matching syntax should be different than what we used earlier. Figure 14.2 presents an implementation for any sequence pattern matching.

```
import scala.xml.Node
object EmbeddedXMLProcessingApp {
   def main(args: Array[String]): Unit = {
      val weatherData =
       <city>
          <name>
             <b>Sunnyvale</b>
          </name>
          <highTemp>80</highTemp>
          <lowTemp>55</lowTemp>
       </city>

      detectXML(weatherData)
   }

   def detectXML(node: Node): Unit = node match {
      case <city>{children @ _*}</city> => {
         println(children)
      }
      case _ => println("No match")
   }
}
```

Fig. 14.2: XML Pattern Matching – Any Sequence

If an XML element contains child elements, we need to use any sequence (_*). This means match the XML element that contains any sequence of child elements. The match output is of type *ArrayBuffer*. In our program, we have several child elements. One of the child elements has an embedded tag in it. So the inner XML structure can vary. When we use any sequence matching, we are telling the pattern matcher that the structure of child elements does not matter, just match the parent tag and return everything embedded by this tag.

14.4 Serialization and Deserialization

Serialization is a process of converting data to XML. One of the situations can be that we have data represented by one or more Scala classes, which need to be sent to the target system in XML format. There are many business cases in industry that require us to transmit data in XML format. Often the structure of XML is seen as a part of the contract between two agents.

```
case class Stock(ticker: String,
      dayMax: Float,
      dayMin: Float ) {
   def toXML =
      <stock>
         <ticker>{ticker}</ticker>
         <dayMax>{dayMax}</dayMax>
         <dayMin>{dayMin}</dayMin>
      </stock>
}

object XMLSerializationApp {
   def main(args: Array[String]): Unit = {
      val appleStock = new Stock("AAPL",145,  152)
      println(appleStock.toXML)
   }
}
```

Fig. 14.3: XML Serialization

Figure 14.3 presents an application that converts typical Scala representation of data to XML format. The class *Stock* is a case class, with three constructor parameters. It has the *toXML* method to convert Scala data to an XML format. The outermost tag is *Stock*, which is also the name of the class. There are three child nodes representing the constructor parameters. Please note how the values are pulled to XML structure using identifiers within curly braces.

In the driver program, we have an object created, with sample values. Next, we call *toXML* on this object, which converts the Scala object to its corresponding XML form. The output of this program is as shown below.

```
<stock>
   <ticker>AAPL</ticker>
   <dayMax>145.0</dayMax>
   <dayMin>152.0</dayMin>
</stock>
```

Deserialization is the reverse of serialization, i.e., converting back from XML representation. In our case, it is converting XML to Scala. This is a common requirement as data transmission is often bidirectional between agents. Let's say two business entities A and B are exchanging business data in XML format. It is common to have bidirectional exchange needs, because there can be several steps in a business flow. In this kind of situation, business A should have both serialization and deserialization capabilities. This is true for business B as well.

This is primarily because the data are processed using some programming languages, on each side. While exchanging, XML format is used as it is programming language independent. Being independent of programming language allows loose coupling between two businesses. Each business can decide what programming language to use based on their convenience.

```scala
import scala.xml.Node
class Person {
   var firstName: String = null
   var lastName: String = null
   var age: Int = 0
   override def toString = firstName+" "+lastName+", "+age
}

object XMLDeserializationApp {
   def main(args: Array[String]): Unit = {
      def xmlData =
         <person>
            <firstName>Charles</firstName>
            <lastName>Darwin</lastName>
            <age>36</age>
         </person>

      println(fromXML(xmlData))
   }

   def fromXML(node: Node): Person = new Person {
      firstName = (node \ "firstName").text
      lastName = (node \ "lastName").text
      age = (node \"age").text.toInt
   }
}
```

Fig. 14.4: XML Deserialization

Figure 14.4 presents an application that takes XML as input data and converts that XML to a corresponding Scala object. We have a class called *Person*, which has three field members. And then it overrides the *toString* method so that the output is readable. On the driver program side, we define a sample of XML data, *xmlData*. We implemented an operation called *fromXML* that takes XML, extracts data, and assigns those data to corresponding fields of a newly created *Person* instance.

When we call *fromXML*, by passing sample XML data, we get a result as an instance of *Person* class. *println* uses the object's *toString* method to print values. The output of this program is as shown below. The output corresponds to our implementation of the *toString* method.

```
Charles Darwin, 36
```

14.5 Loading and Saving

Loading XML from a file is a common operation required in many programming contexts. Most times, XML files are transmitted and persisted. In order to process these persisted files, we need to load them into memory. . I/O operations are slower compared to memory operations; this is one of the reasons why we load data into memory for processing. If the memory is not sufficient, then we need to chunk data and then load the chunks into the memory step wise.

```
class Scientist {
    var firstName: String = null
    var lastName: String = null
    var age: Int = 0
    override def toString = firstName+" "+lastName+", "+age
}

object XMLLoadingApp {
    def main(args: Array[String]): Unit = {
        val scientists =
        xml.XML.loadFile("src/main/resources/Scientist.xml")

        println(fromXML(scientists))
    }

    def fromXML(node: Node): Scientist = new Scientist {
        firstName = (node \ "firstName").text
        lastName = (node \ "lastName").text
        age = (node \"age").text.toInt
    }
}
```

Fig. 14.5: Loading XML

Figure 14.5 presents an application that loads XML data from a file, converts it into a Scala object, and prints data on the console. The class *Scientist* has three field members representing first name, last name, and age. Also we override the *toString* method so that the output is readable, on the console. On the driver program side, we have the *fromXML* method that extracts data from the XML structure and assigns data to corresponding field members of a newly created object of type *Scientist*.

Scala provides a convenient method to load an XML file. The method *loadFile*, as shown in the application, takes the file name and assigns the XML content to the identifier on the left, *scientists* in this case. Now, we have XML in the memory. Next, we call the method *fromXML* by passing this in-memory XML structure. As mentioned earlier, *fromXML* takes the XML apart and assigns values to corresponding fields of a newly created object, which is an instance of the *Scientist* class. The *println* calls the *toString* method of the object, in order to print values on the console. The output of this program is as shown below.

```
Charles Darwin, 36
```

The content of the *Scientist.xml* file is as shown below.

```
<person>
    <firstName>Charles</firstName>
    <lastName>Darwin</lastName>
    <age>36</age>>
</person>
```

```scala
case class Book(title: String,
      author: String,
      price: Double) {
   def toXML = {
      <book>
         <title>{title}</title>
         <author>{author}</author>
         <price>{price}</price>
      </book>
   }
}

object XMLSavingApp {
   def main(args: Array[String]): Unit = {
      val progWithScala = new Book("Programming with Scala",
       "Bhim Upadhyaya", 49.99)

      val xmlData = progWithScala.toXML

      scala.xml.XML.save("src/main/resources/Book.xml",
       xmlData, "UTF-8", true, null)
   }
}
```

Fig. 14.6: Saving XML

Saving the XML structure to a file is another common operation that persists data so that data can be utilized later. It is common practice to create an XML file before transmitting data. Figure 14.6 presents a typical implementation to save XML data. In this application, we have a *Book* class, which has author and price as its constructor parameters. Also it has an operation *toXML*, to convert the Scala representation to the XML equivalent.

On the driver program, first, we create an object of type *Book* and then we call the *toXML* method to get the corresponding XML representation. Then we call the *save* method to save our XML content. The first parameter in the *save* method is the file name, along with the path. The second parameter specifies what encoding to use. The third parameter says whether XML declaration information should be added in the beginning of the file. We are not making use of the last parameter and hence we have the *null* value. The content of the output file, *Book.xml*, is as shown below.

```
<?xml version='1.0' encoding='UTF-8'?>
<book>
    <title>Programming with Scala</title>
    <author>Bhim Upadhyaya</author>
    <price>49.99</price>
</book>
```

14.6 Conclusion

In this chapter, we started with XML literals and demonstrated how XML and Scala code can be intermixed. Then we discussed numerous data extraction operations. Data extraction is a common requirement in many projects, as most of the processing work is done by using some programming languages. We covered a pattern matching technique that helps to match an XML structure that has varying child nodes structures. Next, we discussed serialization, a method that allows developers to convert programming language representation of data to XML format. The reverse of this process is called deserialization, which was covered subsequently. Loading XML from a file is also a commonly required feature. We presented a complete example to load XML from a file. Similarly, we discussed how to persist XML structure using a file.

14.7 Review Questions

1. What is the type of *bookXML*, when the following expression is evaluated?

   ```
   scala> val bookXML = <book>Scala</book>
   ```

2. What is the type of *sum*, when the following expression is evaluated?

   ```
   scala> val sum = <sum>{2+3}</sum>
   ```

3. What is the value and the type of *cityName*, when the following expression is evaluated?

   ```
   val cityName = <city>Sunnyvale</city>.text
   ```

4. What is the output of the following expression?

```
scala> <tag>tag</tag>.label
```

5. What is the output, when the following expression is evaluated?

```
scala> <name><fname>Charles</fname>
 <lname>Darwin</lname>
 </name>.child(1).text
```

6. What is the output, when the following expression is evaluated?

```
<name><fname>Charles</fname><lname>Darwin</lname>
</name> \ "lname"
```

7. Write a code snippet to load an XML file called *Sample.xml* and assign it to a *val* called *sampleXML*.

8. Write a code snippet to save an XML structure called *bookXMLData* without XML definition in the beginning of the file. Use the file name *BookData.xml*.

9. For the code snippet shown below, what is the type of *cities*?

```
case <country>{cities @ _*}</country>
```

14.8 Problems

1. Write a program to find whether a CD with title "Romanza" exists in https:// www.w3schools.com/xml/cd_catalog.xml. If the URL does not exist for your browser, find an XML file online and write a program to detect the existence of one of its items.

2. Write a program to find the food that has the least calories from the online data source https://www.w3schools.com/xml/simple.xml. If the URL does not exist for your browser, find an XML file online that has many child nodes. In your program, make sure you compare at least one item from each child node.

14.9 Answers to Review Questions

1. scala.xml.Elem
2. scala.xml.Elem
3. Value: Sunnyvale, type: String
4. res23: String = tag (*Note: the auto-generated identifier can differ.*)
5. res25: String = Darwin (*Note: the auto-generated identifier can differ.*)
6.

```
res26: scala.xml.NodeSeq =
NodeSeq(<lname>Darwin</lname>)
```

(Note: The auto-generated identifier can differ.)

7.

```scala
val sampleXML = xml.XML.loadFile("Sample.xml")
```

8.

```scala
scala.xml.XML.save("BookData.xml", "UTF-8",
false, null)
```

9. *ArrayBuffer*

14.10 Solutions to Problems

1.
```scala
import java.io.{File, PrintWriter}
import scala.io.Source

object FindingOnlineCDApp {
  def main(args: Array[String]): Unit = {
    val outFileName = "src/main/resources/CDData.xml"
    val cdDataString = Source.fromURL(
      "https://www.w3schools.com/xml/cd_catalog.xml").mkString
    writeToFile(outFileName, cdDataString)

    val cdDataXML = xml.XML.loadFile(outFileName)
    for(a <- cdDataXML.child) {
      if(a.text.contains("Romanza")) {
        println("Corresponding record: "+a.text)
      }
    }
  }

  def writeToFile(fileName: String, content: String): Unit = {
    var printWriter: PrintWriter = null
    try {
      printWriter = new PrintWriter(new File(fileName))
      printWriter.write(content)
    } catch {
      case e: Exception => println("Something went wrong.")
    } finally {
      printWriter.close()
    }
  }
}
```

2.
```scala
import java.io.{File, PrintWriter}
import scala.io.Source

object LeastCaloriesFoodApp {
  def main(args: Array[String]): Unit = {
    val outFileName = "src/main/resources/FoodData.xml"
    val foodDataString = Source.fromURL(
     "https://www.w3schools.com/xml/simple.xml").mkString
    writeToFile(outFileName, foodDataString)

    var foodItem: scala.xml.Node = null; var leastCal: Int
     = 0
    var currentCal: Int = 0; var firstValue = true
    val foodDataXML = xml.XML.loadFile(outFileName)
    for(food <- foodDataXML.child) {
      val cal = (food \ "calories").text.stripPrefix("$")
      if(cal != null && cal != "") {
        currentCal = cal.toInt
        if(firstValue) {
          leastCal = currentCal; firstValue = false }
      }
      if(currentCal < leastCal) {
        leastCal = currentCal; foodItem = food }
    }

    println("Least calories food: ")
    println("Name: "+(foodItem \ "name").text)
    println("Calories: "+leastCal)
    println("Price: "+(foodItem \ "price").text)
  }

  def writeToFile(fileName: String, content: String): Unit = {
    var printWriter: PrintWriter = null
    try {
      printWriter = new PrintWriter(new File(fileName))
      printWriter.write(content)
    } catch {
      case e: Exception => println("Something went wrong.")
    } finally {
      printWriter.close()
    }
  }
}
```

Chapter 15
Parsing

Parsing is a common requirement for industrial projects. It might be required for academic projects as well, depending upon the project type. Often, developers encounter situations which require them to parse special purpose languages or special purpose structures. For example, it is very common to encounter custom JSON structures.

Whatever the reason, it is good to be equipped with parser tools. Scala provides parser libraries that have building blocks which can be used to create parsers and domain specific languages. The major advantage of using a Scala parser library is that we don't have to integrate with any external tool, as far as parsing is concerned. The Scala parser library is the same language, and the output of a parser can be easily integrated with the rest of the programming. It is seamless programming.

15.1 Lexical Analysis and Parsing

Lexical analysis is a process of converting a sequence of characters to a sequence of tokens. These tokens are then analyzed by a parser to find meanings. Let's take an example of an expression, $product = 4 * 5$. Table 15.1 presents tokens for this expression.

Table 15.1: Sample Tokenization

Token	Category
product	Identifier
=	Assignment operator
4	Integer literal
*	Multiplication operator
5	Integer literal

© Springer International Publishing AG 2017
B.P. Upadhyaya, *Programming with Scala*, Undergraduate
Topics in Computer Science, https://doi.org/10.1007/978-3-319-69368-2_15

It is the lexical analysis process that identifies the five tokens shown in Table 15.1. The next thing to identify is whether it is an arithmetic expression, or a logical expression, or something else. Parsing tools can be used to make such identifications. We identify so that we can find the meanings of given data. Once we find the meanings, we can process further. For example, in this case, once we know that it is an arithmetic expression, we can apply the arithmetic operation and get the result. That is the purpose of writing such expressions; we would like to evaluate them.

In the case of complex data, let's say a JSON structure, we would like to extract data so that further action can be taken. Even though a JSON structure looks simple, sometimes it can be heavily nested, making it harder to extract values correctly. Even popular parsers like Google's gson parser may not meet your needs completely. In such a situation, you will need to write your own custom parser using Scala's parser building blocks.

15.2 Creating and Running a Parser

Now, let's create a grammar that is sufficient to handle the expression tokenized in Table 15.1. The left hand side has an identifier called *product* and then we have an assignment operator, followed by an expression. If we would like to parse an expression of the form *product = integer * integer*, then the following grammar should be sufficient.

EXPR ::= TERM * TERM
TERM ::= INTEGER

```
import scala.util.parsing.combinator._

class Prod extends JavaTokenParsers {
    def expr: Parser[Any] = term~"*"~term
    def term: Parser[Any] = wholeNumber
}

object ProductParserApp extends Prod {
    def main(args: Array[String]): Unit = {
        val input = "4 * 5"
        println(parseAll(expr,input))
    }
}
```

Fig. 15.1: Simple Product Expression Parser

Figure 15.1 presents an implementation for the above grammar. You need to include parser combinators dependency in the *build.sbt* file, if you are using an SBT project. A typical value is *libraryDependencies += "org.scala-lang" % "scala-parser-combinators" % "2.11.0-M4"*. There is a trait called *JavaTokenParsers* in the package *scala.util.parsing.combinator*, which contains basic elements. We make use of this trait and implement the grammar. Each production rule becomes a method and its result is *Parser[Any]*. The sequential composition is expressed by the tilde symbol and hence there should be a tilde between two symbols of a production rule.

Once we define a class that contains parsers, we can use those parsers to parse inputs. The method *parseAll* comes from the trait *RegexParsers* and takes two arguments—parser and input. Please note that there are multiple overloaded methods for *parseAll*. The output of the parser is as shown below. We get the message "parsed" and position 6 is the end of the input string, as there are five characters, including white spaces. This means it parsed the input successfully.

```
[1.6] parsed: ((4~*)~5)
```

Now, let's try to parse an ill-formed input, *4 + 5*. It is ill-formed because we have not defined the addition expression. Also we have not defined three-term multiplication. So the input *4 * 5 * 6* is also ill-formed. When we try to parse *4 + 5*, we get the following output. It gives us a message mentioning that it expected '*' but found '+'. Also it points to the correct character, '+'; the index of this character is 3.

```
[1.3] failure: '*' expected but '+' found
4 + 5
  ^
```

15.3 Regular Expression Parser

Regular expression parsers are powerful parsers as they analyze input character by character. These are widely used to analyze character sequences that form some meaningful data for human readers. Figure 15.2 presents an implementation that parses a word and a sentence. A valid word is defined as a combination of characters from 'a' to 'z', including upper cases. A valid sentence is defined as one or more words ending with a full stop; *rep* indicates repetition. Of course, this does not guarantee a valid English sentence, but we supply this definition to get the feeling of a regular expression parser.

The second parser definition, *sentence*, makes use of the first parser definition, *word*. The class *LanguageParser* extends the trait *RegexParsers*, which defines the method *parseAll*. If we want to parse a word type of input, we need to supply a *word* parser. Similarly, if we want to parse a sentence type of input, we need to supply a *sentence* parser. If we supply a *word* parser and a sentence type of input to the method *parseAll*, it will treat the sentence as an ill-formed word. This is because our definition of a word doesn't contain any white space or a full stop.

Similarly, if we supply a *sentence* parser and a word to the method *parseAll*, it will not be able to find all the components of a sentence from our definition of a sentence, and hence will show an error message. The output of this program is as shown below. Both the word and the sentence were parsed successfully.

```scala
import scala.util.parsing.combinator.RegexParsers

class LanguageParser extends RegexParsers {
    def word: Parser[Any] = """([a-zA-Z]+)""".r
    def sentence: Parser[Any] = word~rep(word)~"."
}

object LanguageParserApp extends LanguageParser {
    def main(args: Array[String]): Unit = {
        val wordInput = "sunnyvale"
        val sentenceInput = "Sunnyvale is sunny."
        println(parseAll(word,wordInput))
        println(parseAll(sentence,sentenceInput))
    }
}
```

Fig. 15.2: Regular Expression Parser

```
[1.10] parsed: sunnyvale
[1.20] parsed: ((Sunnyvale~List(is, sunny))~.)
```

15.4 JSON Parser

JSON is a popular data exchange format. If the available parsers don't meet our needs, we end up writing our own parsers. This is not an uncommon situation; even the most sophisticated JSON parsers available from reputed sources may not parse certain JSON data correctly.

Now, let's write a grammar that can parse some JSON data, having an embedded structure. A JSON structure can have key-value pairs within curly braces. There can be multiple values for a particular key, embedded within a pair of square brackets. There can be an embedded JSON structure and so on. We assume that you are familiar with JSON structure, as it is outside the scope of this book.

In the grammar below, we have four production rules. The first rule tries to cover possible combinations. A JSON structure can be a literal or a structure. If it is a structure, it can be one or more elements within curly braces. Also a structure can be another JSON-like structure. Further a structure can be a list of elements separated by commas and embedded within a pair of square brackets. The last rule covers the key-value pair separated by a colon. A key always has to be a string but a value can be either a literal or another structure.

    JSON ::= ENTITY | LIST | STRING | NUMBER
             | "true" | "false" | "null"
    ENTITTY ::= "{" [ELEMENT {"," ELEMENT}] "}"
    LIST ::= "[" [JSON {"," JSON}] "]"
    ELEMENT ::= STRING ":" JSON

Figure 15.3 implements the above grammar. The class *JSONParser* has four definitions, corresponding to four production rules in the grammar. *stringLiteral* and *floatingPointNumber* are members of the trait *JavaTokenParsers* and hence are automatically recognized. The boolean literals and *null* are within double quotes, as we would like to treat them as strings. The reason is that JSON returns these values as strings. The operator formed by combining a tilde sign and a greater than sign means keep right only. If it is turning toward the left, i.e., a combination of a less than sign and a tilde sign, then it means keep left only. We present a table that collects this kind of operator, called *parser combinators*, later in this section.

```scala
import scala.util.parsing.combinator.JavaTokenParsers

class JSONParser extends JavaTokenParsers {
    def json: Parser[Any] = entity | list | stringLiteral |
     floatingPointNumber | "true" | "false" | "null"
    def entity: Parser[Any] = "{"~>repsep(element,",")<~"}"
    def list: Parser[Any] = "["~>repsep(json,",")<~"]"
    def element: Parser[Any] = stringLiteral~":"~json
}

object JSONParserApp extends JSONParser {
    def main(args: Array[String]): Unit = {
      val jsonInput =
        """
        |{
        |   "book" : {
        |     "name" : "Programming with Scala",
        |     "details" : {
        |       "pages" : "250",
        |       "type" : ["Technical","Programming"],
        |       "price" : "USD 49.99"
        |     }
        |   }
        |}
        """.stripMargin

    println(parseAll(json, jsonInput))
  }
}
```

Fig. 15.3: JSON Parser

Now, on the driver program side, we define a sample JSON string. Please note a multi-line string value within three consecutive quotes. Since the object *JSON-ParserApp* extends the class *JSONParser*, the method *parseAll* is available for invocation. When we invoke this method by supplying *json* as a parser and *jsonInput* as a JSON string, we get the following output. The output was manually split into multiple lines in order to fit into the page; originally, it was a single line output. We got the message "parsed", which means the input was parsed successfully. The output is in the form of lists. Table 15.2 presents a collection of operators, including the ones that help to clean up the output so that it becomes more readable. There are many more such combinators available; this table is just to get started. Please refer to the Scala API documentation.

```
[12.7] parsed: List((("book"~:)~List((("name"~:)~
"Programming with Scala"), (("details"~:)~
List((("pages"~:)~"250"), (("type"~:)~
List("Technical", "Programming")), (("price"~:)~
"USD 49.99"))))))
```

Table 15.2: Parser Combinators

Combinator	Description
|	Alternate. E.g.: X | Y
(tilde sign)	Sequential composition.
<~	Keep left
(tilde sign)>	Keep right
opt(P)	Option
repsep(P, Q)	Interleaved repetition
P ^^ f	Result conversion
rep(P)	Zero or more matches of P
rep1(P)	One or more matches of P
repN(n, P)	n matches of P

15.5 Error Handling

The error messages that the combinator parser utility displays are mostly comprehensible. However, it is useful to provide domain specific error messages when we implement a domain specific parser. In this way, the user of the parser becomes much quicker at fixing the problem with the input. Also, Scala can be used as a meta-language to write domain specific languages.

Figure 15.4 presents a simple addition parser that has custom error handling in place. The first production in the addition defines a valid addition. This parser only parses two-operand based addition. If the input does not comply with two-operand addition, then it falls into the failure option, which has a custom message "Invalid input". When an invalid input is supplied, this custom message is printed on the console. The output of the program is shown below.

The error message printed on the console is the one that we provided while defining the parser *expr*. The expression, *6 + 7*, has two operands and there is an infix addition operator. This is as expected. But the starting character, asterisk, is not ex-

```
import scala.util.parsing.combinator.JavaTokenParsers

class AdditionParser extends JavaTokenParsers {
    def expr: Parser[Any] = term~"+"~term |
     failure("Invalid input")
    def term: Parser[Any] = wholeNumber
}

object ParserErrorHandlingApp extends AdditionParser {
    def main(args: Array[String]): Unit = {
        val inputString = "*6 + 7"
        println(parseAll(expr,inputString))
    }
}
```

Fig. 15.4: Parser Error Handling

pected as we have not defined it. There are only two productions. The first defines what constitutes an addition operation, in terms of term. The second production defines what a valid term is. In this case, it is expected to be a whole number.

```
[1.1] failure: Invalid input
*6 + 7
^
```

15.6 Conclusion

We started with the importance of parsing and then discussed lexical analysis and parsing, in general. Then we discussed a simple grammar and its implementation, in order to parse a two-operand product expression. Regular expressions are powerful tools to process input character sequences. We presented a sample regular expression parser to demonstrate the ability to parse input using regular expressions. Next, we presented a JSON parser. JSON is a popular data exchange format and hence the skill to implement JSON parsers is highly desirable. Finally, we demonstrated how to write a custom error message, in a combinator parser.

15.7 Review Questions

1. Name two popular data formats that are used for data exchange in Internet based applications.
2. Parsing comes before lexical analysis. True or false?
3. The method *parseAll* has to be custom implemented. True or false?
4. Why do we write a grammar before we implement a parser?

5. Which trait should be extended in order to implement a regular expression parser?
6. In the code snippet below, what is *sentence*?

```
println(parseAll(sentence,sentenceInput))
```

7. When should we use the combinator *rep(P)*?
8. Which combinator can be used to check the exact number of occurrences?
9. In the following code snippet, how many combinators are there? What is the function of the first and the last combinators?

```
def entity: Parser[Any] =
  "{"~>repsep(element,",")<~"}"
```

15.8 Problems

1. Implement a parser that successfully parses the following expression.

```
(3 + 4) * (2 + 5)
```

2. Implement a parser that successfully parses a two-word sentence, ending with an exclamation sign. Example of valid input: *Hey Bhim!*

15.9 Answers to Review Questions

1. As of this writing, the two popular data formats that are used for data exchange in Internet based applications are XML and JSON.
2. False. Generally, lexical analysis comes before parsing.
3. False. It is available in the trait *RegexParsers*, which is a part of Scala's parser module library.
4. Writing a grammar before implementing a parser gives clarity in thinking. Grammar can be written using paper and pencil. If there is a language, then there is some sort of grammar associated with it. Generally, the accuracy of a language is checked using a grammar and hence it is important to write grammar before writing a parser.
5. In order to implement a regular expression parser, we need to extend the trait *RegexParsers*.
6. In the given code snippet, *sentence* is the name of the parser that this invocation of *parseAll* should be using. Also *sentence* corresponds to a production rule in the corresponding grammar.
7. When we need to check zero or more occurrences of *P*, we should use *rep(P)*.
8. The combinator *repN(n, P)* can be used to check the exact number of occurrences.

9. There are three combinators in the given code snippet. According to Table 15.2, the first combinator causes the opening brace to be thrown away and the last combinator causes the closing brace to be thrown away. This is one of the ways in which we remove unwanted characters from the output of a parser.

15.10 Solutions to Problems

1.
```scala
import scala.util.parsing.combinator.JavaTokenParsers

class ProdOfSumParser extends JavaTokenParsers {
    def expr: Parser[Any] = "("~term~"+"~term~")"~
    "*"~"("~term~"+"~term~")"
    def term: Parser[Any] =
    wholeNumber | failure("Invalid operand")
}

object ProdOfSumParserApp extends ProdOfSumParser {
    def main(args: Array[String]): Unit = {
        val input = "(3 + 4) * (2 + 5)"
        println(parseAll(expr, input))
    }
}
```

2.
```scala
import scala.util.parsing.combinator.JavaTokenParsers

class TwoWordSentenceParser extends JavaTokenParsers {
    def word: Parser[Any] = """([a-zA-Z]+)""".r
    def sentence: Parser[Any] = word~repN(1,word)~"!"
}

object TwoWordSentenceParserApp extends TwoWordSentenceParser {
    def main(args: Array[String]): Unit = {
        val input = "Hey Bhim!"
        println(parseAll(sentence,input))
    }
}
```

References

Boo05. George Boole. *An Investigation of the Laws of Thought*. Gutenberg, `https://www.gutenberg.org/files/15114/15114-pdf.pdf`, Rel. 2005.

Dur88. Peter Duren, editor. *A Century of Mathematics in America*, volume 1. American Mathematical Society, 1988.

Dur89a. Peter Duren, editor. *A Century of Mathematics in America*, volume 2. American Mathematical Society, 1989.

Dur89b. Peter Duren, editor. *A Century of Mathematics in America*, volume 3. American Mathematical Society, 1989.

HBS73. Carl Hewitt, Peter Bishop, and Richard Steiger. A universal modular actor formalism for artificial intelligence. In *International Joint Conference on Artificial Intelligence*, pages 235–245, 1973.

Hod05. Luke Hodgkin. *A History of Mathematics: From Mesopotamia to Modernity*. Oxford University Press, Oxford, 2005.

Kle56. S. C. Kleene. Representation of events in nerve nets and finite automata. *Automata Studies*, pages 3–41, 1956.

OLC17. One laptop per child. `http://one.laptop.org/`, 2017.

Ray65. John C. Raynolds. *COGENT Programming Manual*. Argonne National Laboratory, Argonne, IL, 1965.

UNL13. United nations adult literacy rate. `http://data.un.org/Data.aspx?d=SOWC&f=inID%3A74`, 2013.

© Springer International Publishing AG 2017
B.P. Upadhyaya, *Programming with Scala*, Undergraduate
Topics in Computer Science, https://doi.org/10.1007/978-3-319-69368-2

Index

© Springer International Publishing AG 2017
B.P. Upadhyaya, *Programming with Scala*, Undergraduate
Topics in Computer Science, https://doi.org/10.1007/978-3-319-69368-2

Printed in the United States
By Bookmasters